VOICE
IDENTIFICATION

VOICE IDENTIFICATION
Theory and Legal Applications

By
Oscar Tosi, Ph.D., Sc.D.
Professor, Director
Speech and Hearing Sciences
  Research Laboratory and
Institute of Voice Identification
Michigan State University

University Park Press
Baltimore

UNIVERSITY PARK PRESS
International Publishers in Science and Medicine
233 East Redwood Street
Baltimore, Maryland 21202

Typeset by Photo Graphics, Inc.
Manufactured in the United States of America by the
Maple Press Company

Library of Congress Cataloging in Publication Data

Tosi, Oscar.
  Voice identification : theory and legal applications.

  Bibliography: p. 173
  Includes index.
  1. Voiceprints. 2. Evidence, Expert—United States.
I. Title.
KF9666.5.T67   347'.73'62   78-15786
ISBN 0-8391-1294-7

Contents

Foreword

The development of a methodology by which the human voice, or for that matter subhuman voices, can be identified is not a casual enterprise. Quite to the contrary, it demands first of all a thorough knowledge of the structures and functions of the sound generating system—the vocal apparatus—and with this the understanding of the variability that can occur as signals are produced and reproduced by a vocal system. The differences of acoustic spectra as they are produced by human systems—all of which have unique configurations despite the similarities of structures—constitute yet another set of variables with which to contend. The development of voice identification methodology, which involves electronic voice recording, storage, reproduction, and translation to visual signals, demands not only the complete mastery of the principles underlying the equipment by which the task is to be accomplished but also the mastery of technical skills to accomplish it. Since an integral part of the methodology involves a human being as an identifier, there must also be a thorough understanding of the rationale and demands of the psychophysical task and of the multiphasic aspects of human perception involved in the processing and matching of visual signals.

As a speech scientist and engineer, Dr. Tosi is a person highly qualified to undertake the development of a method by which voices can be identified. He has approached this task with rigor and with a profound sense of the performance capabilities of the set of systems that he has linked together. He has considered both subjective and objective approaches, and can therefore speak authoritatively of the validity and reliability of the results obtained through employment of the method.

The methods of voice identification that he has developed and explicated so well in this book are an outstanding contribution to society. The implications for application of this methodology beyond the forensic arena are far-reaching and demand further study.

Herbert J. Oyer, Ph.D.
Professor of Audiology and Speech Sciences
Dean, The Graduate School
Michigan State University

Preface

This book is intended to satisfy a rather large audience, from lawyers and law enforcement agents to speech scientists, from students of acoustic phonetics and voice identification to persons simply interested in the subject without specific purpose.

To fulfill this scope, a compromise between being too general and descriptive or too particular and scientific necessarily has to be reached. The reader with no background in speech sciences will find most of the text easy to follow if each chapter is studied completely before going to the next. The speech scientist will find this book relevant mainly as an up-to-date reference or monographic source of information on the specific subject of voice identification and elimination.

This book is also intended to be useful to the trial lawyer, either as prosecutor or defense counselor, who will obtain practical data on which to base direct and cross-examinations in dealing with cases involving voice identification or elimination.

Both subjective and objective methods of voice identification were considered; however, special emphasis was placed on the popularly, and wrongly, named "voiceprinting" method because it is the only method presently used for legal evidence. This author, an expert witness on voice identification, refers to this method as "aural and spectrographic examination of speech samples," that is, the aural examination of tape recordings and the visual examination of their spectrograms. This name, if too long, is more representative than the previous one. From the first page of the book, the author wants to emphasize that this subjective aural/spectrographic speech sample examination method is not "infallible" or "foolproof" as some extremist advocates maintain; human error is always possible, as in any other method of identification, or method of anything. However, the author strongly believes that if it is properly used by trained examiners who adhere to the standards set by the International Association of Voice Identification (IAVI) the potential error might become very small, or negligible, to use a word borrowed from differential calculus.

Objective methods are discussed in some detail to offer the reader a clear understanding of their current state of development, the problems the researcher will face when dealing with them, and their excellent possibilities for some time in the future.

A brief history of voice identification and outlooks for the future of voice identification is offered in chapter 5.

Appendix A lists most of the legal cases in which voice identification was offered as evidence in courts of law from December 1970 to the present.

Appendix B lists professional and trainee examiners who can perform voice examination for both the prosecution or the defense and/or offer court evidence if properly qualified by the IAVI.

The author is very grateful to his assistants, Mr. Mark Greenwald and Mr. Hiro Nakasone, who prepared most of the visual materials used in the book. Appreciation is also expressed to Ms. Patricia West, who spent long weekends typing the various drafts of the manuscript.

The author acknowledges with affection the support and encouragement received from his friends, Dr. John W. Black, Dr. Herbert Oyer, Dr. Leo Deal, and Dr. Sadanand Singh. Also, he cordially acknowledges his opponents and cross-examiners in various courts of law, from whom he has learned a great deal.

chapter 1
INTRODUCTION: METHODS OF VOICE IDENTIFICATION

HISTORICAL OUTLINE OF VOICE IDENTIFICATION

Voice identification can be considered a very old or a very modern process, according to the point of view from which it is analyzed. The reason for these two different aspects is that there are multiple methods of voice identification that can be represented along a continuum that goes from the very subjective to the very objective. The oldest method of voice identification is placed at the extreme subjective end of this continuum, i.e., listening to a talker and recognizing him/her through familiarity with his/her voice. This method has been utilized since remote eras, possibly even before the onset of formal language. For thousands of years people have been identifying talkers through their voices by this method with a great deal of certainty. Courts of law in all times and cultures have admitted this type of voice identification evidence as valid, for what it was worth in each particular case. Even the identification of a dog through his bark was admitted in a United States court of law in 1861. In this case, *Wilbur* v. *Hubbard,* the court ruled that, if a person can be identified through his/her voice, the same could be done with the barking of a dog. The owner of the dog, who during the night had killed some sheep of the plaintiff, was forced to pay damages.

The oldest record of this subjective method of voice identification is found in the Bible, Gen. 27:1-22. This case, involving two conspirators, Rebecca and Jacob, and two victims, Isaac and Esau, could be classified in modern jurisprudence as "conspiring to falsely impersonate a person with the purpose of unduly acquiring the rights of primogeniture and dispossessing an individual of his rightful inheritance." This record in the Bible might serve to warn parties interested in voice identification in modern times: even if the decision of the examiner is the correct one, other factors, including bias and lack of confidence in the methods used, could lead to a wrong outcome of the trial. Indeed, Isaac recognized the voice of his son Jacob when Jacob attempted to impersonate his brother Esau; however, Isaac also paid attention to other false evidence (hair on the arms of Jacob astutely supplied by Rebecca) that finally inclined him to wrongly judge.

During the thousands of years that have elapsed since the incident involving Isaac and his sons, no formal study or experiment has been done to obtain laboratory data on the validity of aural identification until fairly recently. In 1935, the famous case *United States* v. *Hauptmann* triggered the attention of scientists to this problem. Hauptmann was accused of kidnapping the son of Colonel Charles Lindberg. In court, Lindbergh recognized the voice of the defendant as being the same as the voice of the person who demanded a ransom of him by telephone. Hauptmann was found guilty and condemned to death. Because this voice identification was one of the main pieces of evidence for that verdict, a controversy arose after this case. People questioned the validity of voice identification, an important factor in the defendant's eventual death sentence. Dr. Frances McGehee, professor of psychology at Johns Hopkins University, performed an experiment on voice identification by aural means (1937), an experiment that attempted to bring scientific insight into the relative validity of the process.

Certainly, the listeners in her experiment were no experts and the method utilized was the only one available up to that date; i.e., *aural identification by the long-term memory process.* In this method the listener possesses stored information on the perceptual features of a talker's voice, such as pitch, melodic pattern and rhythm, quality, and respiratory group. When he/she listens to a voice on a second occasion, this information is retrieved from his/her mind and it is compared with similar features of the present talker. Then the listener decides whether or not it is the same voice as the one stored in his/her memory.

Moving toward the more objective end of the continuum, the modern aspects of voice identification started after World War II with electronic developments like the tape recorder, the acoustic spectrograph, and more recently the computer. These developments have generated new methods of voice identification and have resulted in the presence of the expert witness in voice identification in a court of law.

In this introductory chapter an overview of the different methods of voice identification, the types of errors that could be produced, and standard nomenclature in voice identification are offered. Subsequent chapters deal with the acoustic basis of speech as a scientific background to voice identification, discussions on the different methods available in this field, a report on actual legal cases involving voice identification evidence, the roles of the different persons in a court of law, the present controversies in voice identification, and a look toward the future of voice identification.

TYPES OF TESTS AND ERRORS
IN VOICE IDENTIFICATION AND ELIMINATION—
CONTEMPORARY AND NONCONTEMPORARY SAMPLES

A classification of the different methods that can be used to identify or eliminate an unknown talker as being the same as one of several known talkers is portrayed in Figure 1.1. It should be emphasized that these methods are not exclusive, i.e., two or more of them can be used simultaneously in practical, case-related examinations.

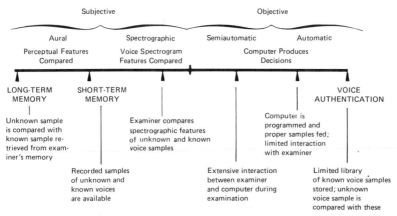

Figure 1.1. Voice identification methods, ranked from the most subjective to the most objective.

Methods of voice identification and elimination can be classified into two general groups: subjective methods and objective methods. The meaning of the words subjective and objective might vary for different persons. However, for the author, in the context of voice identification they can be operationally defined as follows: subjective methods of voice identification are those in which decisions are produced by the human mind; objective methods are those in which decisions are produced by mechanical or electronic means. However, it is necessary to point out that in these objective methods there still exists a great deal of human interaction, because, for example, the computer has to be programmed and its results have to be interpreted by an examiner.

Also, it should be noticed that all methods of voice identification form a continuum, as shown in Figure 1.1. The aural identification of "live" voices of talkers out of the sight of the listener is the most subjective end of this continuum; the computer *authentication* of a talker who claims his voice is the same as one out of a small library of talker's voices stored in the computer's memory bank is the most objective end of this continuum.

Typically, all types of aural examination of voices and visual examination of speech spectrograms for purposes of voice identification or elimination should be considered subjective methods, although the latter is closer to the objective part of the spectrum of methods than the former. Semiautomatic (requiring extensive human interaction) and automatic (requiring limited human interaction) computerized methods of voice identification are considered objective, but the former is closer to the subjective part of the scale than the latter. Whether subjective or objective, voice examinations for legal purposes always require the intervention of an examiner, at the very least to prepare the samples, to interpret the results from the computer, and to testify in court. It must be remembered (as already stated) that computers will perform only according to the data input and programming produced by a human.

According to the composition of unknown and known voice samples, tests of voice identification or elimination can be classified into three groups: discrimination tests, open tests, and closed tests. In the *discrimination tests* the examiner is provided with one unknown voice sample and one known voice sample. He has to decide whether or not both samples belong to the same talker. Two types of errors can be produced in the discrimination tests: (a) false elimination, when the examiner decides that both samples belong to different talkers, but they are actually from the same talker; and (b) false identification, when the examiner decides both samples belong to the same talkers when they actually do not.

In the *open tests* the examiner is given one unknown voice sample and several known voice samples. He is told that the unknown sample may or may not be found among the known samples. This type of test can yield three types of errors. The first is false elimination, when the unknown voice sample *is* among the known samples, but the examiner decides that it is not. The second and third types are errors of false identification that can originate from two possibilities: (a) one of the known samples is the same as the unknown one, but the examiner selects the wrong one; and (b) none of the known samples is the same as the unknown one, but the examiner decides that one of them is the same as the unknown.

In the *closed tests* of voice identification the examiner is also given one unknown voice sample and several known voice samples but he is told that the unknown voice sample is also included in the known voice samples. Consequently, here only one type of error can be produced: an error of false identification in which the examiner selects the wrong known sample.

In the three types of tests discussed the examiner may choose to include a self-confidence rating with each decision, according to a scale—for instance:

1. Very uncertain that my decision is correct
2. Fairly uncertain that my decision is correct
3. Fairly certain that my decision is correct
4. Almost certain that my decision is correct

These confidence ratings allow the plotting of the so-called receiver operating characteristic, which is described in Chapter 3 ("Receiver Operating Characteristic" section).

In addition, an examiner can be allowed to express no opinion in case of doubt. This is not a common procedure in laboratory experiments, but is the normal practice of professional examiners, as discussed "in extensis" through the different chapters of the book. Because the implications of errors of false identification are so different than those of false elimination for practical applications, they should always be reported in the laboratory experiments performed. A simple statement of the percentage of correct identifications obtained in an experiment does not describe results properly.

NOMENCLATURE USED IN VOICED IDENTIFICATION TESTS

In the literature of voice identification some words and phrases have acquired precise meanings with which the reader must become familiar before proceeding further. Definitions of the most commonly used specific words and phrases in such literature follow.

Trials of voice identification: synonymous with "tests of voice identification," i.e., experiments of any kind done with such purpose, mainly within a laboratory or a controlled situation, where the "unknown" sample is from a person known to the experimenter. The use of the word "trial" has no legal implications.

Intratalker variability: refers to the change of acoustic characteristics of the same word when uttered on different occasions by the same talker. This change can be due to a variety of reasons—physiological, psychological, etc.

Intertalker variability: refers to the different acoustic characteristics of the same word when uttered by different talkers.

Number of utterances: refers to the number of repetitions of the same clue word taken from the same subject. Different utterances of the same word are useful for surveying the range of intratalker variation.

Contemporary samples: those multiple speech samples obtained from the same talker during the same recording session.

Noncontemporary samples: those multiple samples obtained from the talker during different recording sessions. In practical situations unknown (criminal) voice samples and known (suspect or defendant) voice samples are noncontemporary.

Phoneme: any basic sound or "building block" of a language; different combinations of phonemes result in the different words of a language, according to the traditional phonetic sciences. English is composed of approximately 44 phonemes.

Grapheme: any written symbol that might represent a phoneme; a letter of a particular alphabet. Normal English spelling is based on the Roman alphabet and composed of 26 graphemes. "Phonetic" alphabets, such as the International Phonetic Alphabet, include one grapheme for each phoneme to be written (see Table 1, Chapter 2).

Clue words: any identical or similar words of speech samples from unknown and known talkers that are used for comparing their voices.

Open tests: those tests of voice identification in which the examiner is told that the unknown voice sample may or may not be included among the known voice samples. He has to decide whether or not the unknown sample is one of the known ones and if he decides positively, must determine which known talker is same as the unknown.

Closed tests: those tests of voice identification in which the examiner is told that the unknown voice sample is included among the known voice samples. He has to decide which known sample is the same as the unknown one.

Discrimination tests: those tests of voice identification in which the examiner is provided with voice samples from an unknown talker and voice samples from only one known talker. He has to decide whether or not the unknown sample is the same as the known one.

Match trials: those experimental open or discrimination tests of voice identification in which the experimenter has included a voice sample from the unknown talker among the known talker voice samples.

No-match trials: those experimental open or discrimination tests of voice identification in which the experimenter has not included a voice sample from the unknown talker among the known talker voice samples.

chapter 2
ACOUSTICS, PHONETICS, AND THEORY OF VOICE PRODUCTION

A CYBERNETIC MODEL OF VOICE COMMUNICATION

Before entering into a description of voice identification methods, it seems convenient to discuss briefly some basic phonetics, acoustics, and the theory of speech production. First a cybernetic model of voice communication is introduced (Figure 2.1).

Normally three elements are present in a voice communication situation: the talker, the transmission medium, and the listener, as represented in this model. The box symbolizing the talker is further divided into three compartments or levels: (1) a psycholinguistic level where a verbal message (idea) is generated; (2) a physiological or neuroanatomical level where a series of neuromotor (electric) pulses, codified and correlated with the psycholinguistic message at the Broca's area of the cortex and other neural centers, is produced and fired to activate the muscular structures of the vocal tract; and (3) an acoustic level where speech waves, correlated with the series of motor pulses and hence with the message, are formed by proper modulation of the air stream from the lungs. This modulation is obtained by modifying resonances of the vocal tract cavities through movements of its muscular structures as activated by the neuromotor pulses (articulation).

All these transductions from one level to the next occur with a short delay between each transduction. The output from each level controls the input by a feedback loop, as portrayed in the model. These multiple feedback loops are a basic device in any system ruled by cybernetic laws, as the voice communication system is.

The final product of the talker's vocal tract is a speech signal, codified according to a phonetic and linguistic pattern that varies,

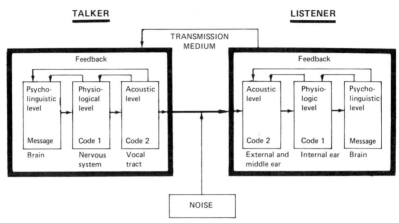

Figure 2.1. A cybernetic model of voice communication. Both the talker's and the listener's processes in voice communications can be classified according to three levels: psycholinguistic, physiological/anatomical, and acoustic. Feedback loops control all stages. Noise in this model signifies any factor that interferes with intelligibility of the message.

of course, for each language and dialect. As can be deduced from this model, the final acoustic signal includes the output of the psycholinguistic and neuroanatomical levels of speech production.

This speech signal (a longitudinal acoustic wave) propagates through a medium with a constant velocity (the velocity of propagation of sound in that medium) in all directions. Eventually this vibration or acoustic speech signal reaches the hearing structures of the listener, where the process described for the talker is inverted in order to decode the original message. The medium of propagation of the speech signal might comprise several steps and transductions, such as air, a telephone line, and a tape recorder, and the intelligibility of the message may be deteriorated by noise factors. Also, feedback loops regulate the hearing mechanism and the talker/listener interaction, as portrayed in the model.

In addition to a phonetic content the acoustic speech signal also includes talker-dependent features that can be used to identify or to discriminate one talker from another. A critical problem in the talker identification process is detecting features that are strongly talker-dependent in order to develop efficient parameters of identification. Sets of efficient parameters vary according to the type of method used for talker identification. However, these parameters are difficult to detect and to list, even when using subjective methods of voice identification. For instance, a listener might be able to identify a familiar voice with great reliability; however, he would be unable in many instances to describe and list the features he has used to produce this voice identification, in the same way that any observer can identify subjectively the face of a person, but a great difficulty would arise if that observer were asked to describe or list the features he used to produce such a face identification.

Because the acoustic level of the talker's speech, i.e., the resulting sound wave, is the sole material available to identify a talker among others through their voices, a discussion of phonetics, acoustics, and the theory of production of speech is necessary prior to entering specifically into the description of methods of voice identification.

BASIC PHONETICS

Voice identification deals with speech, i.e., the speech sounds of a given language. The different sounds of a language are produced by the phenomenon of *resonance,* as discussed in futher detail in the "Acoustic Speech Production" section in this chapter. Resonance demands the existence of at least two acoustic systems: a primary source of sound energy and a resonant system. There are three of these primary sources of acoustic energy in human speech: the glottal source, the frictional source, and the plosive source.

The glottal source is the "raw" sound or buzz produced by vibration of the glottis, or vocal folds, which transmits such vibration to the stream of air expelled by the talker's lungs.

The fricative source is the noise-like sound produced by the turbulences of that stream of air when it is forced through any constriction of the talker's vocal tract. The plosive source is also a noise-like raw sound originated by the release or explosion of air when the speaker first closes the vocal tract and then suddenly opens it. Either of these two sources can be used independently or in conjunction with the glottal source, according to the instantaneous phonetic needs of the talker.

These primary sources provide a type of "raw sound," with only a few variable characteristics, that could not serve to build a phonetic code or language. The necessary variations for such a purpose are provided by the resonant vocal tract of the talker, which modifies at each instant the sound characteristics of the primary sources.

The vocal tract consists of a series of cavities and structures: the trachea; the pharynx; the mouth, containing the velum or soft palate, the tongue, the teeth, and the lips; and the nasal cavities.[1] The position or shape of these structures, called *articulators,* can be modified at any instant by a series of coordinated gestures (*articulation*). Generally each articulatory gesture modifies by resonance the characteristics of the primary sound, producing a speech wave as an output from the vocal tract. This speech wave, modulated according to a phonetic code or language, conveys a message to the listener.

Any language is composed of a number of elemental sounds, called *phonemes,* that combine to produce the different words of that language, according to the classic although now obsolete description of the phonetic sciences. English is formed by approximately 44 phonemes. Phonemes are classified into vowels, glides, semivowels, and consonants.

A vowel is defined as a continuant sound (it can be produced in isolation without changing the position of articulators), voiced (using the glottis as a primary source of sound), with no friction (noise) of air against the vocal tract passage. There are approximately 16 vowels in English. These English vowels are classified according to the position of the greatest arching point of the tongue for producing them. Considering the vertical plane, vowels are produced in a high, middle, or low position of that arching point of the tongue from hard palate down. Considering the horizontal plane, vowels are produced in a front, mid, or back position of the greatest arching point of the tongue. Figure 2.2 presents a diagram of the articulatory classification of vowels.

A semivowel has the continuant and voiced characteristics of a vowel, but some degree of friction or noise accompanies its production. In English there are two semivowels symbolized by the letters /l/ and /r/.

Glides can be defined as vowel-like sounds, differing from the vowels in a lack of the continuant characteristic: glides are produced rather during a fast dynamic change of the articulators; the first

---

[1] The nasal cavities can be coupled to the vocal tract by the opening of the velum or soft palate; this happens for the nasal sounds such as *m, n,* and *ng.* Also, some "nasalized" vowels are produced with this coupling. Because nasal cavities are of constant shape for nearly all talkers, nasal sounds provide a good reference for voice identification (Su, Li, and Fu, 1974).

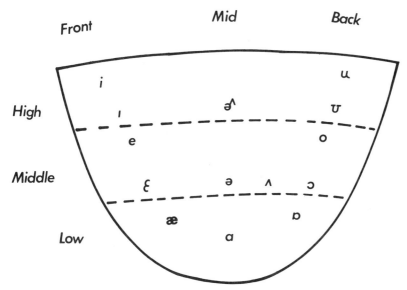

Figure 2.2. Diagram of articulatory classifications of English vowels, according to the relative position of the greatest arching point of the tongue when producing these vowels in isolation.

sounds of the word "you" and the word "what" provide examples of glides.

Consonants are phonemes other than vowels or glides. Consonants always include friction and they can be classified into voiced or voiceless, and fricative, plosive, affricative, or nasal according to the manner of production.

Voiceless consonants are those produced with no glottal vibration; friction of air from the lungs of the talker against a constriction of his vocal tract is the only source of primary sound or acoustic power for this type of phoneme (/s/, /f/, and /t/ are examples of voiceless consonants). Voiced consonants use both glottal vibration and friction of air as primary generators of sound (/z/, /v/, and /d/ are examples of voiced consonants).

According to the manner of production, consonants can be fricatives, plosives, affricatives, or nasals. Fricatives are continuous sounds produced in isolation with no changes of articulatory positions, like the sounds represented by the grapheme /s/ in the word "single" and the grapheme /z/ in the word "zoo." Plosive consonants are those produced by closing the vocal tract at some point, building air pressure and then releasing that air suddenly or exploding it. In English there are six plosives, three voiced and three voiceless, symbolized by the graphemes /b/, /d/, /g/ and /p/, /t/, /k/, respectively.

Affricative consonants are composition consonants, formed by a fricative followed by a plosive. In English there are two affricatives; the first sounds of the words "judge" and "church" are the voiced and the voiceless English affricatives, respectively.

Nasal consonants are those produced with the resonance resulting from the conjunction of the nasal cavities and the vocal tract cavities. This is accomplished by opening the velum or soft palate. There are three nasal consonants in English, symbolized by the graphemes /m/, /n/, and /ng/, as in the words "mother," "concave," and "sing," respectively.

From the point of view of placement of the tongue and lips for producing consonants (points of articulation) they can be classified as bilabial, labio-dental, alveolar, palatal, and velar.

The acoustic characteristics of the same phoneme vary slightly with every actual utterance by a talker. Each particular variation of a phoneme is called an *allophone*. A phoneme should then be considered as an ideal model with average characteristics drawn from the accepted range of its allophonic variations.

It should be clear to the reader that to speak does not mean to utter a series of concatenated phonemes. Phonemes constitute only an abstraction used successfully by phoneticians from remote times up to the present. Modern phonetic schemes consider the flow of speech as a variable set of concurrent distinctive features, such as voice, friction, nasality, etc. However, the phonetic transcription of a speech sample is useful for many purposes, including voice identification. In all cases the voice identification examiner should be aware that the written symbols or letters of the sample voice transcript constitute only a gross approximation of the actual sounds of the speech analyzed. The same phoneme might vary considerably, according to the particular talker and the particular neighboring phonemes within the sample considered. This influence on a phoneme or on a syllable by the preceding and following sounds is called coarticulation.

A *grapheme* is any written symbol or letter that represents a phoneme in a transcription. A system of graphemes is called an alphabet. A logical alphabet for a given language would be one that consists of as many graphemes as there are phonemes in that language, i.e., each grapheme univocally representing each phoneme. But unfortunately this is not the case in many languages, usually due to the fact that they have inherited the Roman alphabet for writing. English, a language born within one of the Roman provinces, was not an exception to this fact. Although the 26 or so letters of the Roman alphabet fit very well to the more or less equal number of phonemes in Latin or the Romance languages (Italian, Spanish, Rumanian, etc.), they are obviously insufficient to properly represent the 44 English phonemes. The spelling troubles of this language, illogical to the degree of hideousness, originate in the lack of a proper English alphabet composed of 44 letters, one for each English phoneme.

As a result of this and similar problems (consider the language with no written form), several alphabets have been created to simplify the phonemic transcription of English or any other language. One of these alphabets is the International Phonetic Alphabet. Table 1 presents that alphabet. The reader seriously interested in voice identification is encouraged to become familiar with this alphabet.

ACOUSTICS

Sound in general and speech sounds in particular are mechanical vibrations or recurrent movements of a body, for instance, particles of air, within an elastic medium. The number of recurrences per second is called the frequency (f) of the sound. A period (τ) is the duration of one recurrence of the vibrating mass. Period and frequency of any vibration or sound are in an inverse relationship, i.e., the longer the period, the smaller the frequency. In mathematical symbols:

$$\tau = \frac{1}{f}[\text{sec}]$$

$$f = \frac{1}{\tau}[\text{Hz}]$$

The intensity (I) or acoustic power of a sound is proportional to the square of the maximum displacement (*amplitude*) of the vibrating particle around a neutral position of equilibrium within the elastic medium. Intensity or power is perceived as loudness; usually it is measured in decibels (dB), which is a logarithmic ratio between

Table 1. The Phonetic Alphabet

Symbol	Spelling	Spoken form	Symbol	Spelling	Spoken form
Vowels					
i	bee	bi	ɝ	further	ˈfɝðɚ *accented syllable only, r's sounded*
ɪ	pity	ˈpɪtɪ			
e	rate	ret			
ɛ	yet	jɛt	ɜ	further	ˈfɜðɚ *accented syllable only, r's silent*
æ	sang	sæŋ			
a	bath	baθ *as heard in the East, between æ (sang) and ɑ (ah)*	ɚ	further	ˈfɜðɚ *unaccented syllable only, r's sounded*
ɑ	ah	ɑ			
	far	fɑr			
ɒ	watch	wɒtʃ *between ɑ (ah) and ɔ (jaw)*	ə	further	ˈfɜðɚ *unaccented syllable only, r's silent*
ɔ	jaw	dʒɔ		custom above	ˈkʌstəm
	gorge	gɔrdʒ			əˈbʌv *unaccented syllable*
o	go	go			
ʊ	full	fʊl			
u	tooth	tuθ	ʌ	custom above	ˈkʌstəm
					əˈbʌv *accented syllable*
Diphthongs					
aɪ	while	hwaɪl	ju	using	ˈjuzɪŋ
aʊ	how	haʊ		fuse	fjuz
ɔɪ	toy	tɔɪ	ɪu	fuse	fɪuz
Consonants					
p	pity	ˈpɪtɪ	dʒ	jaw	dʒɔ
b	bee	bi		edge	ɛdʒ
t	tooth	tuθ	m	custom	ˈkʌstəm
d	dish	dɪʃ	m̩	keep 'em	ˈkipm̩
k	custom	ˈkʌstəm	n	vision	ˈvɪʒən
g	go	go	n̩	Eden	ˈidn̩
f	full	fʊl	ŋ	sang	sæŋ

Table 1.   (*continued*)

Sym-bol	Spelling	Spoken form	Sym-bol	Spelling	Spoken form
Consonants (*continued*)					
v	vision	ˈvɪʒən		angry	ˈæŋ·grɪ
θ	tooth	tuθ	l	full	fʊl
ð	further	ˈfɜðə	ļ	cradle	ˈkredl
s	sang	sæŋ	w	watch	wɒtʃ
z	using	ˈjuzɪŋ	hw	while	hwɐɪl
ʃ	dish	dɪʃ	j	yet	jɛt
ʒ	vision	ˈvɪʒən	r	rate	ret
h	how	haʊ		very	ˈvɛrɪ
tʃ	watch	wɒtʃ		far	fɑr
	chest	tʃɛst		gorge	gɔrdʒ

This is reproduced by permission from *A Pronouncing Dictionary of American English*, © 1953 by G. & C. Merriam Co., Publishers of the Merriam-Webster Dictionaries.

the intensity of the sound being measured and a given reference, usually the threshold of hearing at 1,000 Hz. The formula for calculating this ratio is expressed as:

$$dB = 10 \log_{10} \frac{I}{I_0}$$

where I is the sound intensity (in watts/m²), and I_0 is the standardized reference intensity, usually 10^{-12} watts/m². A human ear in optimal conditions can perceive as a sound vibrations from 20 to 20,000 cycles per second or Hertz (Hz), providing that the intensity is above a given threshold.

Frequency is perceived as a pitch: in general, the higher the frequency the higher the perceived pitch. The frequency range of speech sounds goes approximately from 100 to 7,000 Hz, but most information of speech, including talker-dependent features, is found within a range of 100 to 4,000 Hz.

Another parameter of the sound wave is the wavelength (λ); it is the distance covered during one period by a wave or disturbance propagating within a medium from a source (i.è., a talker) to a receiver (i.e., a listener). The velocity of propagation (c) is a constant that depends on the medium. For air in normal conditions it is approximately 340 m/sec. The definition of wavelength can be expressed in mathematical symbols as follows:

$$\lambda = c\tau = \frac{c}{f}$$

It is clear from this relationship that the higher the frequency of a sound the shorter its wavelength is.

Sounds can be classified into two large groups: simple and complex. A *simple sound* is produced by a special recurrent movement of any mass, called simple harmonic motion (SHM). The path or trajectory of a SHM vibration is a straight line. This vibration is maintained by elastic central forces, that is, forces of a magnitude proportional to the *elongation,* or displacement of the vibrating masses from a neutral position. Maximum displacement to either side of the neutral position is called *amplitude.* SHM is depicted by a sinusoidal graph in a *time domain* plot, that is, a graph in which time is plotted on the horizontal axis. On the vertical axis, elongation, or displacement, intensity, or other equivalent parameters of sound, can be plotted (Figure 2.3, a_1 and a_2). Due to the shape of the curve obtained in plotting this type of graph (a sine curve), the SHM is also called a *sinusoidal wave.* However, it should be remembered that the trajectory or path of the vibrating particle in SHM is a straight line. A simple sound or sinusoidal wave is perceived by a listener as a pure tone with a pitch relative to the frequency. A tuning fork or an audiometer are sources of pure tones.

The same type of vibration can be expressed in the *frequency domain* (spectrum) rather than in the time domain (Figure 2.3, b_1 and b_2). A frequency domain plot is a graph in which frequency is plotted on the horizontal axis. Intensity, amplitude, or other parameters of the sound (for instance, phase) can be plotted on the vertical axis. Because for a constant SHM there is only one frequency of vibration, the frequency domain plot or spectrum of this wave will consist of only one line at the particular frequency of the sound considered. The length of such a line will portray, according to a graphic scale, the parameter of that sound plotted on the vertical axis, i.e., the intensity of that sound. It should be understood that the spectrum considered here is one correlated with a steady, periodic sinusoidal wave of indefinite duration.

A *complex sound* is one that is not simple or sinusoidal. All speech sounds are complex. A complex sound wave can be periodic, quasi-periodic, or aperiodic. In the periodic complex wave each cycle is completed during the same time or period; in the aperiodic waves duration of each recurrency is random (Figure 2.4). Quasi-

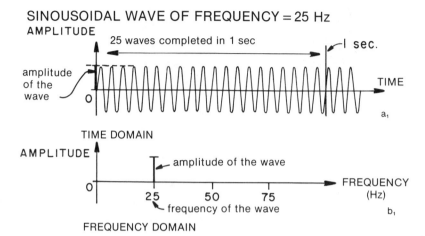

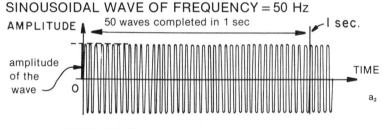

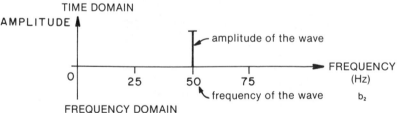

Figure 2.3. Mathematical plottings of sinusoidal waves: a_1, a_2) time domain; b_1, b_2) frequency domain.

periodic complex waves are those in which the period of every cycle is not constant but the difference is rather small. All voiced sounds of speech are correlated with quasi-periodic complex waves. An exception might be the steady portion of a sustained vowel sung by a trained opera singer, which is fairly periodic. Complex sounds can be portrayed in the frequency domain by their spectra as well as by their time domain waves. Because spectra are closely related to most methods of talker identification, a discussion on spectra is offered in the section on Fourier Transforms.

20

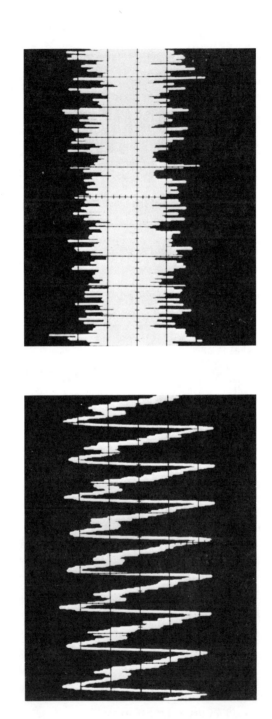

/z/   /s/

Figure 2.4. Time domain plottings of a quasi-periodic wave (the sound /z/) and an aperiodic wave (the sound /s/).

Fourier Analysis

The French mathematician and physicist Fourier discovered last century that any complex steady and periodic sound can be decomposed into a set of simple or sinusoidal waves of different frequencies and intensities. As an illustration of this principle, Figure 2.5 shows a complex wave decomposed into four simple or sinusoidal sounds, called *harmonics* of the complex sound. This graph presents the waves in the time domain. The frequency of the first harmonic, or fundamental frequency, coincides with the frequency of the complex wave. The frequency of the other harmonics are integer multiples of the first harmonic. For instance, assuming that the frequency of the complex wave is $F_0 = 200$ Hz, the frequency of its first harmonic f_1 is also 200 Hz. The frequency of the second harmonic is $f_2 = 2 \times 200$ Hz; the frequency of third harmonic is $f_3 = 3 \times 200$ Hz, etc. In general:

$$f_n = n f_1$$

where f_n is the frequency of the nth harmonic and f_1 is the frequency of the first harmonic ($f_1 = F_0$).

Computation of intensity or amplitude of each harmonic of any complex sound can be accomplished by three alternative methods:

1. By calculation, using the Fourier algorithms
2. By laboratory procedures, using analog instruments, such as variable filters, analyzers, or spectrographs
3. By computer, properly programmed with the Fourier algorithms

The number of harmonics composing a complex wave is theoretically infinite, but in practical usage just a few harmonics, usually about 20, can yield an acceptable approximation of the actual complex wave analyzed. It should be noted that at any instant the elongation or displacement (or any quantity plotted on the vertical axis) of the complex wave is the algebraic sum of the elongations of all the harmonics at the same instant; i.e., in Figure 2.5 the elongation of the complex wave at the instant $t = 5.3$ msec is:

$$ij = ab + cd + ef + gh$$

It should be understood that if the same harmonics are shifted along the horizontal axis of time, that is, if their *phases*[2] are

---

[2] Phase is the amount of time, or equivalent angle ($\tau \equiv 360°$), represented by the shift of a sinusoidal wave along the horizontal axis of time to obtain a zero ordinate at zero time.

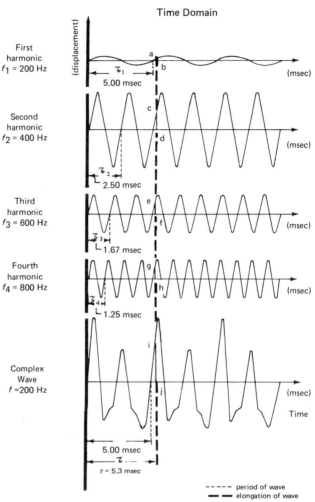

Figure 2.5. A complex periodic wave, decomposed into four harmonics (sinusoidal waves) and presented in the time domain, according to the Fourier theorem. The period or frequency of the complex wave is the same as the period or frequency of the first harmonic. Elongation *ij* of the complex wave at any instant, (in the example, *t* = 5.3 msec) is the sum of elongations *ab, cd, ef,* and *gh* of the component harmonics at the same instant. Phase of each harmonic in this example is 0.

changed, the shape of the complex wave, obtained by adding point by point the elongations of each harmonic, will change. Therefore, for some applications it is important to know the phase of each harmonic. (The phase of each harmonic in Figure 2.5 is 0.) It seems that in speech or voice identification this characteristic is not important.

Fourier analysis is the operation of decomposing the complex wave into its sinusoidal harmonics; Fourier synthesis is the inverse operation, that is, adding all the harmonics together to rebuild the complex wave. This last procedure is used to produce artificial computer speech; it is also employed to study acoustic characteristics of speech by a research method called "analysis by synthesis."

A mathematical expression of the Fourier analysis is the so-called Fourier Expansion:

$$v(t) = c_0 + \sum_{n=1}^{\infty} c_n \sin n\omega t + \varphi_n$$

or alternatively:

$$v(t) = c_0 + \sum_{n=1}^{\infty} a_n \cos n\omega t + \sum_{n=1}^{\infty} b_n \sin n\omega t$$

where:

$v(t)$ = values of the successive vertical ordinates v (amplitudes, intensities, pressures, etc.) of a complex periodic wave, expressed as a function of time t

c_0 = a vertical axis constant term (amplitude, intensity, pressure, etc.). If the complex wave is symmetrical in reference to the horizontal axis of time, then $c_0 = 0$

c_n = peak ordinate (amplitude, intensity, pressure, etc.) of the nth harmonic in the sin Fourier expansion

$\sum_{i=1}^{n}$ = summation of a series of similar terms that differ from each other only by the value n. For the first term it is $n = 1$, for the second term $n = 2$, and so on until the last term is added to the series

n = number of the harmonic considered

ω = angular frequency of the periodic complex wave $\omega = 2\pi F_0$

φ_n = phase of the nth harmonic, or the time or equivalent angle (period $\equiv 360°$) obtained by shifting the sinusoidal wave along the horizontal axis to obtain a zero ordinate at zero time

a_n = peak ordinate of the nth harmonic in the cosine term of the cos-sin Fourier expansion

b_n = peak ordinate of the nth harmonic in the sine term of the cos-sin Fourier expansion

Also:

$$c_n = \sqrt{a_n{}^2 + b_n{}^2}$$

and

$$\varphi_n = \frac{\tan^{-1} b_n}{a_n}$$

where:

$$c_0 = \frac{1}{\tau} \int_{-\frac{\tau}{2}}^{\frac{\tau}{2}} v(t)\,dt$$

$$a_n = \frac{2}{\tau} \int_{-\frac{\tau}{2}}^{\frac{\tau}{2}} v(t) \cos n\omega t\,dt$$

$$b_n = \frac{2}{\tau} \int_{-\frac{\tau}{2}}^{\frac{\tau}{2}} v(t) \sin n\omega t\,dt$$

Fourier Transforms

Because a complex steady wave can be decomposed (or expanded) as a summation of sinusoidal waves (harmonics of the complex wave), it is convenient to express these harmonics as spectrum (in the frequency domain) rather than in the time domain. Figure 2.6 portrays the same waves presented in Figure 2.5 but in the frequency domain. Here each line is the spectrum of one of the sinusoidal or harmonic components of that complex sound. Therefore, the spectrum of a complex periodic wave, steady and temporarily unlimited, consists of several lines, each one representing a simple sound (sinusoidal wave) or harmonic component. The corresponding mathematical expression, called the Fourier Transform, is as follows:

$$V(\omega) = \int_{-\infty}^{\infty} v(t)e^{-j\omega t}\,dt$$

where:

$V(\omega)$ = the values of the successive ordinate V of the spectrum of a complex wave as a function of angular frequency ω

$v(t)$ = the values of the successive ordinates v of the wave expressed as a function of time t

The Fourier Transform provides the value $V(\omega)$ of each ordi-

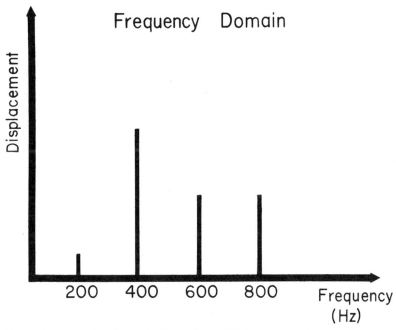

Figure 2.6. Same Fourier analysis as Figure 2.5, but portrayed in the frequency domain. Each discrete line of this graph represents the frequency and amplitude of each component harmonic. The whole graph is the theoretical spectrum of the complex wave.

nate of the spectrum for each angular frequency $\omega(\omega = 2\pi f)$ along the horizontal axis.

Similarly, knowing the spectrum $V(\omega)$ of a complex wave, it is possible to convert to the time domain by use of the Inverse Fourier Transform:

$$v(t) = \frac{1}{2\pi} \int_{-\infty}^{\infty} V(\omega) e^{j\omega t} d\omega$$

Notice that $e^{-j\omega t} = \cos \omega t - j \sin \omega t$ and $e^{j\omega t} = \cos \omega t + j \sin \omega t$. (These are the Euler's "magic formulas.")

For those readers who do not have a mathematical background, a brief explanation of the symbols included in the Fourier formulas might be useful.

The sign $\int_{-\frac{\tau}{2}}^{\frac{\tau}{2}}$ is called a "definite integral within the limits $\frac{\tau}{2}$

and $\dfrac{-\tau}{2}$.'' Integration is one of the two operations of infinitesimal calculus, the other one being differentiation. Differentiation is related to the "differential" dt, which is essentially (for our purposes) a small interval of time tending to zero (but never reaching that limit). Integration can be interpreted as a summation of very small rectangles formed by the base dt, the function under the integral and two lateral ordinates. This summation includes the total area between the two abscissa values indicated at the integral sign, in our case from $\dfrac{-\tau}{2}$ to $\dfrac{\tau}{2}$.

The letter j in the exponent $e^{j\omega t}$ stands for the "imaginary" unit $\sqrt{-1}$. It simply indicates values to be plotted on the axis of the ordinates. For instance, the complex number $4 + 5j$ determines a point in the plane XY of which the coordinates are: 4 on the axis of the abscissas (horizontal) and 5 on the axis of the ordinates (vertical).

So much for spectra (either discrete or continuous) of steady sounds. But the ongoing speech signal is a variable wave in the time domain. Two types of spectra can be derived from a portion of this variable temporal speech signal—a succession of short-term spectra or a long-term spectrum.

A *short-term spectrum* is the spectrum of a very short segment (25 msec or so) of the speech signal; this short segment could be considered quasi-steady, i.e., including very minor changes in the speech wave. Therefore, a one- or two-minute portion of the speech signal will generate a succession of short-term spectra. This succession of short-term spectra is shown in a spectrogram.

Specifically, a spectrogram is a graphic display obtained by an instrument called an acoustic spectrograph or by a digital computer properly programmed. The spectrogram shows time in addition to frequency or intensities within each band of frequencies. That is, the spectrogram portrays the successive short-term spectra of a flow of sound, such as ongoing speech, or the duration of the spectrum of a constant sound. Time is plotted on the horizontal axis of the spectrogram; frequencies on the vertical axis. Intensities are portrayed by the degree of darkness of the spectrographic patterns represented (bar spectrograms) or by isobaric lines (contour spectrogram). Each type of phoneme presents a characteristic pattern in its spectrogram, including both phonetic and talker-dependent features information (Figure 2.7a and b).

Commercial spectrographs have a selection of 45 Hz and 300 Hz scanning filters bandwidth. If 45 Hz is selected a "narrowband" bar spectrogram displaying the harmonics of the input speech sample is obtained (see Figure 2.8a). 300 Hz will yield a "broadband" bar spectrogram displaying the formants of the vowels and the higher power bands of the consonants (Figure 2.8b). Isobaric lines of a contour spectrogram are plotted every 6 dB (Figure 2.8c).

The *long-term spectrum* is an average spectrum of the whole one- or two-minute speech signal (Figure 2.9). It should be understood that both short-term spectra and a long-term spectrum include not only phonetic information but also talker-dependent features; therefore, they are used for talker identification. It should also be stated that spectra are influenced by the recording channels and the analyzing instruments; however, in some cases this influence can be eliminated.

It is important to understand that any analyzing device interacts with the processed sound. Indeed, Fourier analysis performed by instruments essentially consists of the outputs of filters of given bandwidths. These filters scan through the complete range of frequencies of the analyzed complex sound, allowing only the power within each filter bandwidth to pass. The output from the analyzer will therefore indicate the acoustic power of the complex wave within each complete filter bandwidth, but will not contain an indication as to the particular frequency or band of the complex wave that actually contains that power. In sum, each type of analyzer would yield a different spectrum from the same input wave, according to the bandwidth of its analyzing filters.

Euclidean Distance

In the section in Chapter 3 on "Objective Methods of Voice Identification," Euclidean distances are discussed as they are used in voice identification. A brief explanation will clarify this concept for the reader without mathematical background.

Assume a plane xy; each point of that plane is determined by two coordinates; for example $A(x_A, y_A)$ or $B(x_B, y_B)$. The actual distance (or Euclidean distance) between the two points, $A(x_A, y_A)$ and $B(x_B, y_B)$ is:

$$d_{AB} = \sqrt{(x_B - x_A)^2 + (y_B - y_A)^2}$$

(Figure 2.10). If, rather than by two coordinates, the space studied

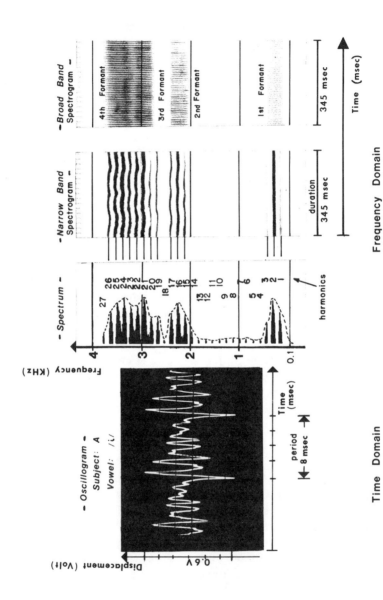

Figure 2.7a.

28

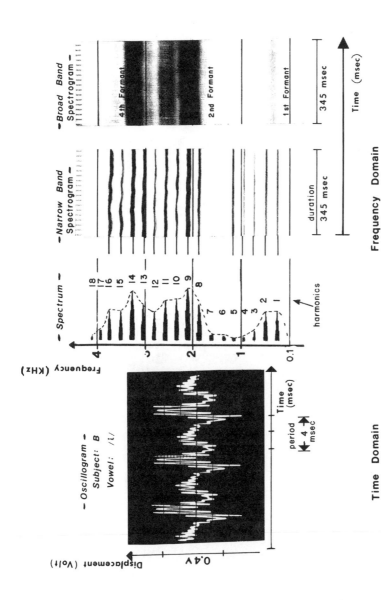

Figure 2.7a and b. Oscillograms (time domain), spectra, and spectrograms of the vowel /i/ uttered by two different talkers, A and B.

29

30

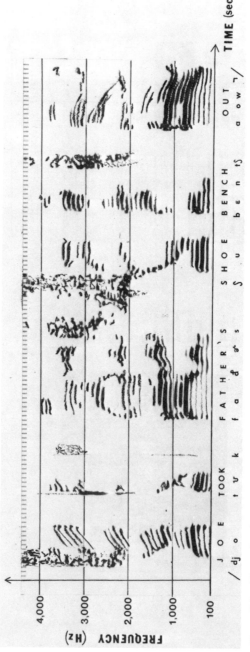

Figure 2.8a. Narrowband spectrogram of the sentence "Joe took father's shoe bench out."

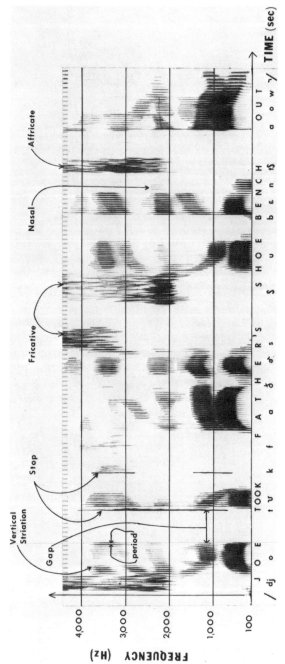

Figure 2.8b. Broadband spectrogram of the sentence "Joe took father's shoe bench out." Characteristic patterns and formants are labeled.

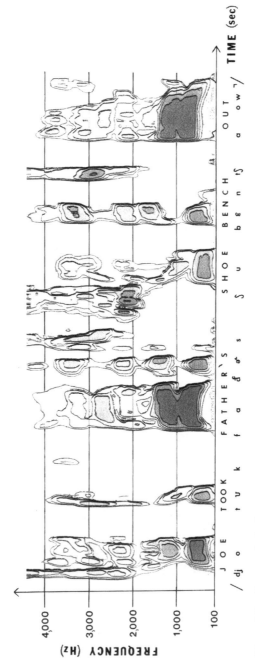

Figure 2.8c. Contour (isobaric) spectrogram of the sentence "Joe took father's shoe bench out."

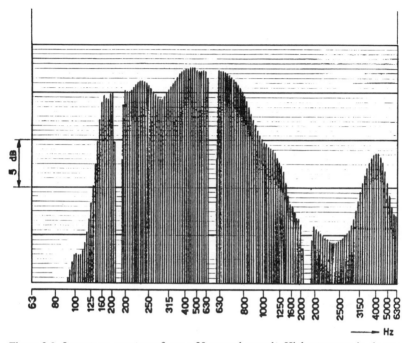

Figure 2.9. Long-term spectrum from a 20-second speech. Highest power is shown at the 500 Hz region.

is represented by n coordinates, the distance between the two points $A(\overbrace{x_A, y_A, \ldots, z_A}^{n})$ and $B(\overbrace{x_B, y_B, \ldots, z_B}^{n})$ is:

$$d_{AB} = \sqrt{(x_B - x_A)^2 + (y_B - y_A)^2 + \ldots \ldots (z_B - z_A)^2}$$

(Of course, a space of more than three coordinates has no geometric representation.) Coordinates may be generalized to any kind of parameters, not necessarily length. They could be mean frequencies of formants, glottal frequency, slopes of speech transients, etc. In any case, d_{AB} computed with the equations indicated above is called the "Euclidean distance between A and B."

A brief example will illustrate the use of Euclidean distance with speech parameters. Assume that the unknown and known voice samples of the phoneme /i/ are to be compared through the Euclidean distance between the mean frequencies of first and sec-

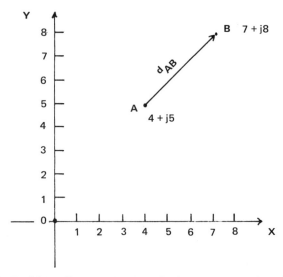

Figure 2.10. Euclidean distance or vector d_{AB} between two points A and B of coordinates ($x_A = 4$; $y_A = 5$) and ($x_B = 7$; $y_B = 8$). Coordinates can be also expressed as complex numbers ($4 + j5$; $7 + j8$) where $j = \sqrt{-1}$ (imaginary unit). The "real" term is plotted along the x axis; the "imaginary" term is plotted along the y axis. Quantities and units of these coordinates might be of any type, not necessarily length.

ond formants of this pair of phonemes (the measured or "extracted" parameter in this case). Further assume that the mean frequency of the first formant of the unknown voice sample (F_1) is 230 Hz, the mean frequency of the first formant of the known voice sample (F_1') is 250 Hz, and the second formants' mean frequencies are respectively $F_2 = 2{,}100$ Hz and $F_2' = 2{,}300$ Hz. Euclidean distance in this two-dimensional space will be:

$$d = \sqrt{(F_1' - F_1)^2 + (F_2' - F_2)^2}$$
$$= \sqrt{(250 - 230)^2 + (2300 - 2100)^2}$$
$$= 201 \text{ Hz}$$

These concepts can be extended to any number of dimensions and any kind of parameter. A criterion can be established to decide whether or not the voices are from same or different talkers, according to statistical data on the expected magnitude of Euclidean distances from the voice of the same person uttering the same sound on a noncontemporary basis.

ACOUSTIC SPEECH PRODUCTION

A talker has available two primary sources of sound to produce speech: the glottal source (vibration of the glottis) and the frictional source, that is, the noise-like sounds produced when air from the lungs is forced through a constriction of the vocal tract (to produce fricatives or affricatives) or is suddenly released (to produce plosives). The spectrum of the glottal source, the buzz-like sound produced by the vibration of the glottal folds, consists of a discrete series of lines, each representing a sinusoidal wave, spaced by an integer multiple of the fundamental frequency; the amplitude of these discrete components or harmonics of the spectrum decays in a linear fashion at a rate of about 12 dB per octave. Its range of frequencies is approximately from 60 Hz to 7,000 Hz. Perception of pitch from a talker is mainly due to the fundamental frequency of the first harmonic of the glottal source. The spectrum of a glottal source is represented in Figure 2.13a(α).

The spectrum of the frictional source is continuous; that is, it does not consist of harmonics discretely spaced but of sinusoidal waves of all frequencies within the speech range, approximately from 60 Hz to 7,000 Hz. The amplitude or intensity of these continuous components is approximately even (Figure 2.13b(α)).

These two sources, glottal and frictional, can be used successively or simultaneously by the talker during ongoing speech, according to instantaneous phonetic needs. The simultaneous use of the glottal and frictional sources originates the voiced consonants (such as /z/). The exclusive use of the frictional source of speech originates the voiceless consonants (such as /s/). Vowels (periodic or quasi-periodic waves) are correlated with discrete spectra. Voiceless consonants (aperiodic waves) are correlated with continuous spectra. Voiced consonants (periodic or quasi-periodic waves) have a mixed spectra (discrete and continuous).

The flow of variable spectra that constitutes the acoustic speech signal is produced by each talker by utilizing the various articulators (mandible, tongue, soft palate, etc.) in various combinations to obtain particular resonances from the primary generators of sound;

that is, the glottal vibration and the friction of the stream of air from the lungs. Clearly, different spectra (associated with the different sounds of speech or phonemes) are produced by the phenomenon of resonance in the vocal tract (amplification of some components of the source sounds and damping of other components).

To establish a phonetic code, i.e., to speak, the spectra of the sources are modified (some bands of frequencies are amplified, some are damped) at each instant by resonance in the vocal tract. The modification produced is determined by the talker through articulatory movements. Each position of the articulators produces the desired phonetic spectrum that conveys a semantic meaning to the listener, as well as information on a talker's characteristics.

In these spectra the relative position of the frequency bands of relatively higher amplitude convey the perception of different consonants. There are also frequency bands of relatively higher amplitude in the spectra of vowels, called formants. The positions of the center frequency of these higher amplitude bands or formants in the spectrum are numbered according to their relative values, as F_1, F_2, F_3 . . . F_n. The formants' bandwidths, their relative amplitudes, and their transitions determine the different phonetic elements, as well as the talker-dependent features, necessary for voice identification. However, these parameters are variable not only among different talkers, but also within the same talker's utterances of the same phonetic elements. Coarticulation is one important factor responsible for intratalker variations (Daniloff and Hammarberg, 1973; Stevens, House, and Paul, 1966). Table 2 presents the average center frequencies of formants and their relative intensity of 5 steady or isolated Italian vowels as uttered by 12 talkers.

To have resonance at least two acoustic systems are necessary: a source or generator of sound power and a resonant system. The latter will amplify some harmonic components of the source sound and will damp some other harmonics, giving a particular shape or envelope to the spectrum of the instantaneous output of sound. The different envelopes of the spectra of complex sounds determine the qualities or characteristics of a particular sound. An illustration of different spectra envelopes associated with different vowels is presented in Figure 2.11. In general the envelope of each spectrum is correlated both with a particular phoneme and with the talker; it is largely independent of pitch.

The particular envelope of the spectrum of a sound includes both a phonetic content and the individual characteristics of each

Table 2. Average mean frequencies (Hz) and relative intensities (dB, relative to the intensity of F_1 of /o/) of formants F_1, F_2, and F_3 of five Italian vowels, uttered in isolation by twelve adult male talkers

Formant	/i/		/e/		/a/		/o/		/u/	
	Hz	dB	Hz	dB	Hz	dB	Hz	dB	Hz	dB
F_3	2800	(−28)	2700	(−28)	2200	(−30)	2600	(−36)	2300	(−40)
F_2	2100	(−19)	1800	(−12)	1100	(−4)	600	(−6)	650	(−17)
F_1	240	(−3)	300	(−2)	600	(−2)	300	(0)	230	(−3)

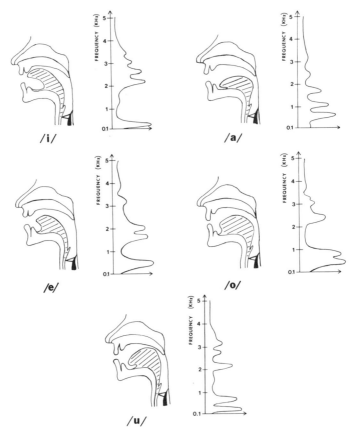

Figure 2.11. Different positions of articulators to produce five vowels in isolation. These articulations are correlated with different response or resonance curves; combined output spectrum of power source and resonance curve conveys the perception of each phoneme, plus the individual speech characteristics of the talkers.

talker. Indeed, the talker-variable spectra of the output of ongoing speech carries not only semantic information but also talker-dependent features. Therefore, most methods of talker identification or elimination are based in some way on elements of the temporal acoustic spectra.

Figure 2.12a presents spectra of the vowel /a/ produced by the same talker, using two different glottal frequencies or pitches. Note that in either case the peaks of power of the spectra formants fall at approximately the same mean frequencies (600 Hz, 1,100 Hz, and 2,200 Hz) irrespective of fundamental frequencies. Figure 2.12b

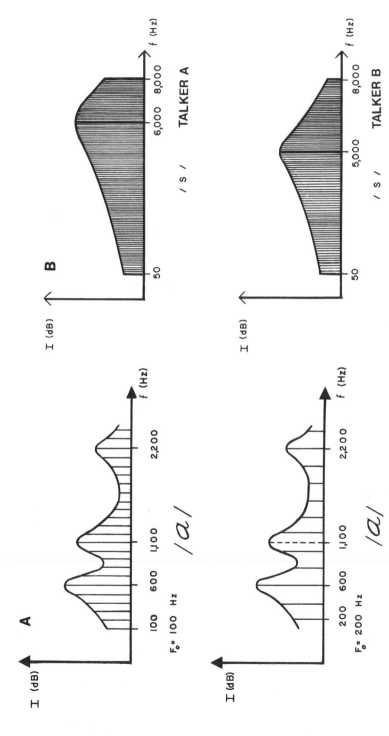

Figure 2.12. a. Spectra of the phoneme /a/ produced by the same talker, using glottal frequencies of 100 Hz and 200 Hz, respectively. Note that formants are approximately at the same regions in both cases. b. Spectra of the phoneme /s/ uttered in isolation by two talkers. Note different center frequencies of high power bands for each individual.

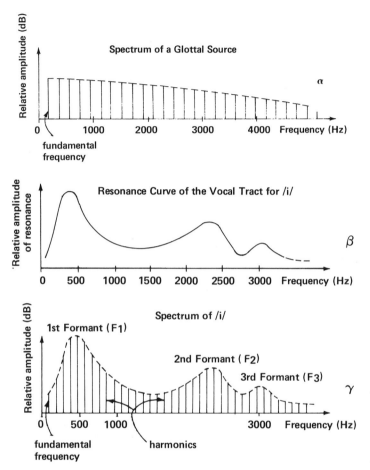

Figure 2.13a, b. Discrete spectrum (γ) of a voiced phoneme produced by resonating a glottal source (α) in the vocal tract (β).

is a similar presentation of the spectra of the consonant /s/ uttered by two talkers (see also Figures 2.7a, b).

Mathematically, the process of resonating a primary source of a sound in the vocal cavity of the talker, can be expressed by the following equation (Stevens and House, 1961):

$$V(\omega) = U(\omega) \cdot T(\omega) \cdot R(\omega)$$

where:

$V(\omega) =$ the instantaneous output spectrum from the talker's mouth; that is, the intensity of the spectrum at each fre-

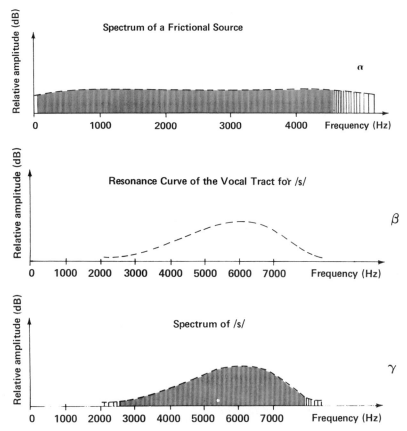

Figure 2.13b. Continuous spectrum (γ) of a voiceless phoneme produced by resonating a friction source (α) in the vocal tract (β).

quency. The letter ω stands for each frequency f (or rather angular frequency, $\omega = 2\pi f$) within the range of frequencies considered

$U(\omega)$ = the spectrum of the glottal source; intensity as a function of angular frequency ω

$T(\omega)$ = the resonant curve or transfer impedance of the talker's vocal tract, at a given configuration. T is the particular ordinate value of resonance for each frequency ω

$R(\omega)$ = the influence on the phoneme considered by the radiation from the talker's lips, at each frequency ω

This equation is illustrated by Figures 2.13a and b. In those figures the factors $T(\omega)$ and $R(\omega)$ are included in the vocal tract resonant curve.

Both the glottal spectra and the resonance curves produced by a vocal tract depend on anatomic and organic characteristics as well as on the functional or behavioral process used by each person during the learning stages of speaking.

SPEECH ACOUSTIC PARAMETERS AND SOURCES OF VARIABILITY OF VOICE IDENTIFICATION SAMPLES

The most general acoustic parameters of speech are time, frequency, and intensity distribution within all bands of frequency, simultaneously present in the instantaneous talker output; in other words, the parameters portrayed by a spectrogram. Comparisons of these general or derived spectral/temporal parameters are the basis of all talker identification systems, both subjective and objective. One source of variation of these spectral parameters depends on phonetic content. In systems of voice identification tests in which it is desirable to minimize the phonetic source of variability, comparisons of the unknown and known voices are performed by using only similar sample sentences produced by the talkers. The problem is that, even maintaining a constant text, values of the selected phonetic parameters will differ not only among different talkers, but also will vary within the same talker if different utterances of the same text are compared. The first type of variation is called *intertalker variability*; the second type is referred to as *intratalker variability*.

Researchers of voice identification have searched for sets of efficient acoustic parameters, i.e., parameters that convey the least intratalker variability and the most intertalker variability possible in all conditions that may occur in normal or even in disguised speech. These efficient sets of parameters are to be selected according to the particular method of voice identification explored; that is, optimal selection of parameters for aural examination could not be adequate for visual examination of spectrograms or for automatic voice identification.

One recent study searching for efficient parameters in automatic talker identification was conducted by Wolf (1972). He selected the following parameters as optimal for his method: fundamental frequency at given locations of the sample sentences, amplitude of filtered vowels, mean frequencies of formants F_1 and

F_2 in given locations of the sample sentences, spectrum slope at a given location of vowel /u/, high frequency spectrum envelope characteristics at the middle of the voiceless consonant /s/, etc.

Atal (1972) selected pitch contours as optimal parameters for a particular method of automatic talker recognition.

For the method of visual examination of spectrograms the following parameters were considered (Tosi et al., 1972): mean frequencies and bandwidths of vowel formants, gaps and type of vertical striations, slopes and transients of formants, duration of similar phonetic elements and plosive gaps, energy distribution of fricatives and plosives, and interformant acoustic density patterns.

For the aural examination method, perceptual parameters and voice-attribute rating elements, such as pitch, rate, intensity, and quality, have been used by Holmgren (1967).

However, even if efficient parameters are properly selected, it should be understood that to identify or eliminate an unknown talker as being the same as a known one, for legal purposes, is a complex operation involving more than a method and efficient parameters. Indeed, four well-defined phases or elements should be considered in the complete process: (a) the talkers themselves; (b) the transmitting and recording channels; (c) the system of identification, including examiners and machines used for that purpose; and, finally, (d) the presentation of voice identification evidence in court, including direct and cross-examinations of expert witnesses by prosecutors and defense counselors, and the reaction of the jury and the judge to the presentation of this type of evidence. All these elements could interact negatively with the correct final legal judgment of talker identification or elimination.

At this point in time there exists no comprehensive laboratory experimentation covering the effects of all the elements mentioned. Only partial, uncoordinated controlled data are presently available on some of these elements. To supplement these restricted controlled data, several extrapolations and considerations might play a role in ensuring the validity of voice identification in a court of law. The variability introduced by the talkers themselves and by the recording channels might yield no-opinion decisions or false eliminations rather than false identifications, which is acceptable in our system of justice (i.e., it is preferable to decide that a criminal is innocent rather than that an innocent is guilty). The training and experience of examiners, enhanced by data that they have collected through years of practice, might supply the necessary foundation to render validity to their decisions. Thorough knowledge of the subject by the law officers involved in the presentation of voice identification evidence in court, the presence of adversary expert witnesses, and proper admonitions by the court to the jury might give the proper weight to this type of evidence, preventing the jury from becoming unduly impressed by the testimony of a given expert witness and consequently making the wrong decision.

With these ideas in mind, a discussion of the variability in speech samples introduced by the talkers themselves and by the transmitting and recording channels follows.

Variability Produced by the Talkers Themselves

Even assuming a population of homogeneous talkers, that is, talkers of the same dialect of a given language, the same age, and the same background group, intertalker variability has basically two sources: (a) the anatomical and physiological differences existing among different persons; and (b) the learned speaking differences among different persons.

In the section on "Acoustic Speech Production" it was explained that speech is produced by resonance in the talker's vocal tract. The notion that no two similar things are ever equal is almost a natural law; the reader would easily accept that finding two absolutely equal faces is a very remote possibility. Finding two absolutely equal vocal tracts should be considered as remote a possibility, even if vocal tracts are not so readily visible as faces are. The conclusion that logically follows is that different vocal tracts necessarily have to produce different resonances or speech spectra, differences significant for voice identification purposes.

In addition to these anatomical differences, every person "experimentally" develops an individual and unique process of learning to speak, although these processes are generally similar. The uniqueness of the process contributes to the building of unique speech spectra for each individual when uttering a given word. This learned difference is dramatically illustrated by persons speaking a non-native language.

Actually there is no controversy concerning intertalker variability other than possible confusion arising when two people's speech is very similar. A more important problem is produced by the intratalker variability; that is, the variability of speech spectra between two utterances of the same words produced by the same talker. Are these intratalker variabilities lesser than or different than the intertalker variabilities? The whole problem of talker identification and elimination could be basically centered in the reliable answer to this question. Two alternative types of research might find such an answer, at least tentatively: (a) inference through a substantial number of laboratory tests using any method but testing speech samples from "unknown" talkers who are known to the experimenters, because errors committed by examiners in these tests might bring controlled data on which to base the inference; and (b) definition of optimal parameters from spectral/temporal speech samples that can be proved to be invariant for the same talker's speech but highly variable for different talkers' speech.

Both ways have been tried by researchers: Tosi et al. (1972) tried inference through controlled testing and Wolf (1972) tried to define optimal parameters. Still more experimentation with controlled data is necessary to eliminate controversy in this area.

On the other hand, there is no problem in the identification of sources of intratalker variability. The commonly accepted sources are: (1) time elapsed between pairs of utterances from the same talker; (2) anatomical, physiological, and psychological circumstantial conditions of the talker; (3) manner of utterance; and (4) disguising or mimicking attempts by the talker.

Concerning the time elapsed between two utterances of the same words from a talker, there exist some experimental data that suggest the magnitude of the acoustic change due to this factor. In one experiment (Tosi et al., 1972), it was found that a one-month lapse between recordings of similar samples from the same talker increased the errors of false identification and false elimination approximately 10% with respect to the same type of errors yielded by comparing contemporary samples from the same talkers. However, it is necessary to interpret these results with caution, because the examiners in that experiment were forced to always give a positive decision. An option to give no-opinion decisions could have lowered that increase of errors due to time elapsed between sample voices. Another danger to be avoided in interpreting these results is to make fast, obviously nonvalid linear extrapolations, as was done by a defense counselor in a legal trial where the author was an expert witness. During a cross-examination that counselor asked: "If during the lapse of one month your error increased about 10%, during the six months elapsed between the recordings of the questioned voice samples and the defendant's samples, the error will increase to 60%. Is this not so?" This author's reply was: "No, I do not think so, sir, because in keeping with your linear extrapolation criterion a lapse of 24 months would yield an impossible error of 240%."

Endress, Bambach, and Flosser (1971) published a paper dealing with speech spectrogram changes due to age, voice disguise, and voice mimicking. Concerning change due to age, these authors stated that the pitch of 7 subjects recorded over up to a 29-year period shifted to lower frequencies and their ability to vary the pitch of their speech decreased. The authors only disclosed data from 1 subject, stating that this was a typical example. Furthermore, they stated that the materials used were available magnetic tape recordings of several politicians and actors made through the years.

Several criticisms can be made of this study. First, there was no information on how and where the magnetic tape recordings were produced and kept. Stretching of tapes through the years might introduce changes in the pitch; this observation actually came from the audience when the authors first presented the study at the 79th meeting of the Acoustical Society of America (April 1970). The situation, place, and mood of a politician or an actor might also induce changes of pitch. A third criticism is that the data were not properly presented in the paper, except for the talker called "B." In addition, only in the summary and not in the text of the paper was the number of talkers used disclosed. The failure of the authors to present a table with data from all talkers produces some confusion in the interpretation of results.

In contrast to this study, the writer has recordings of his own voice over a lapse of 27 years, from very young adulthood to the present. No change in pitch has been detected.

Concerning the voice disguise part of the same study, Endress, Bambach, and Flosser used 5 male talkers and 1 female talker reading the same text in five different conditions: undisguised voice, changed pitch, changed rate, different accent, and different dialect. The authors observed that the structure of the formants of the phonemes /a/, /i/, and /m/ was altered according to the type of disguise. This conclusion confirms a fact very well known to examiners of voice identification, who are aware of the alterations in normal spectrographic patterns produced by some defendants who try to disguise their voices in some way at the moment of recording "known" samples. Usually the pitch is lower in that circumstance than in the unknown samples; consequently, the mean frequencies of the formants could also be affected. However, there are several aspects of spectrographic patterns other than formant structures known to professional examiners that are unlikely to change noticeably by voice disguising, such as gap durations of plosive sounds, that Endress, Bambach, and Flosser did not consider in their study. Implications for practical cases of the reported alterations on voice identification are not significant, because examiners will usually make a no-opinion decision in a case where the unknown sample differs from the known ones for any reason, including disguising. At worst a good job of disguising could lead to a false elimination rather than to a no-opinion decision from the examiner, which still is compatible with our system of justice. With respect to mimicking, materials for the Endress, Bombach, and Flosser study consisted of impersonations of five public figures by "two well-known German imitators." Their conclusion was that these imitators "succeeded in varying the formant structure and fundamental frequency of their voices, but they were not able to adapt these parameters to match, or even be similar to, those of the imitated persons" (1971).

This conclusion is based, of course, on the abilities of two professional imitators, but it coincides with the opinion of several scientists, including Kersta (1962b), who disclosed spectrograms of a speech made by President Kennedy and copied by his imitator, Elliot Reid. There were obvious differences in the spectrograms, despite the fact that, according to Kersta, the voices sounded extremely similar. If the conclusions from these different authors can be trusted, the real danger to voice identification by speech spectrograms, mimicking, is minimized. If spectrographic patterns of mimicked speech differ from the imitated person's patterns, a voice identification examiner can hardly be misled into making a false identification. In the decision concerning the case of *California* v. *Law* (1972), the court considered the danger of mimicking, and consequently acquitted the defendant because there existed some presumption of such a possibility in that particular case. It should be noted that the writer, as an expert witness in that case, pointed out to the court the potential danger of good mimicking (Siegel, 1976).

New longitudinal experiments on the subject of time elapsed between voice samples are being conducted. So far, matching of noncontemporary samples (about 2 years' lapse) from the same talker has not supported the notion of substantial changes (Smrkovski, 1976). More controlled data are necessary to completely clarify this source of intratalker variation; such data can be obtained only in the future by using current recorded samples of a population of talkers for comparison.

Concerning the anatomical, physiological, and psychological sources of variability of speech samples from the same talker, there exists almost no controversy. Everyone does agree that this source can originate variability in different degrees, from drastic ones in cases of pathology or trauma in vocal tract structures, to minor ones in cases of psychological stress of whatever form. Again, experimentation in this area is only fragmentary and inconclusive.

Manner of utterance of speech samples is also a source of intratalker variability. When word samples from a talker reading a text are compared with similar words uttered in spontaneous speech, considerable variability should be expected. Normally, readings are produced with better articulation and a lower pitch than spontaneous speech. There is no available controlled experimental data in this area, that is, comparing readings with spontaneous speech, for voice identification purposes. However, there exist data from practical cases. In most instances the voice identification examiner has to compare the spontaneous speech used by the unknown talker with readings of the same text made by defendants. However, in many practical cases the defendant is requested to repeat sentences rather than to read sentence by sentence from the textual transcript of the criminal call. The officer in charge utters one single sentence from that text and requests the defendant to repeat the same words after him. Recordings of the known samples continue in this manner until the whole transcript is completed. This procedure represents a compromise between reading and spontaneous speech, and also tends to diminish attempts at faking by the defendant.

A related matter concerns matching the same words from different phonetic contexts. Coarticulation affects spectral characteristics of the same words or sounds if taken from different contexts. Hazen (1973) performed an experiment using this type of material. He found that attempts at matching the same five words taken from different contexts yielded only 26% correct identification. This percentage was increased to 80% when comparing words extracted from the same contexts, keeping all other conditions of the experiment invariant. Hazen used physically excerpted portions of spectrograms containing only the clue words and employed no properly trained examiners for this rather small experiment (280 trials in total). However, it was a useful test that yielded laboratory data to corroborate what should not be done in practical situations.[3] It should be noted that professional examiners do not physically excerpt words from a spectrogram, as Hazen did, because transients carry relevant information. In addition, they certainly use more than five words in practical cases, taken from the same contexts as uttered by unknown and known talkers, in order to eliminate coarticulation effects.

Disguising the voice by any of several means might introduce considerable variability in speech samples. The method used and/or the skill of the examiner might or might not overcome this type of variability, but if he is allowed to render a no-opinion decision as to whether the samples compared came from the same or from different talkers, the number of errors can decrease drastically as compared with a situation in which the examiner is forced to give a positive decision in all cases tested.

Hollien and McGlone (1976) experimented with disguised voices, obtaining results indicating that in only 23.3% (on the average) of the 150 open trials performed comparing disguised voices of 24 talkers with their normal voices was a correct identification possible. They forced the examiners to give a positive decision (either identification or elimination) in all tests. In addition to the experiment itself, the authors discussed in their paper its implication for the "voiceprint" method, concluding that because the results from this study have proven that such a technique is not resistant to disguise it should be discarded from legal usage.

This suggestion might be a most reasonable one if voice examinations in legal cases were conducted according to conditions employed in this experiment. Because this is not the case, their suggestion should be critically analyzed before being considered. Essentially, what Drs. Hollien and McGlone are suggesting is that samples from different talkers, distorted by disguise in this case, and by noise, characteristics of recording channels, psychological, and physiological variations in other cases, tend to become similar and that they are used in practical cases to always (in 100% of the cases examined) render a positive identification. Neither of these two assumptions were proven by these authors, and, in the opinion of this author, they are actually not correct. Indeed, a professional

---

[3] More information on Hazen's study is offered in the section on "Visual Examination of Speech Spectrograms" in Chapter 3.

voice examiner, acting within standards of competency and honesty, simply will not use distorted samples for legal examinations, or at least he will not use such samples to make positive identifications.

However, noncontemporary samples, including disguise or other types of distortions, either produced by different talkers or by the same talker, tend to be different, not equal as suggested in this experiment. In such a case, different samples can lead only to a no-opinion decision or at the worst to a false elimination, but obviously they cannot lead to a false identification unless the examiner is not properly trained. Therefore, it logically follows that the concern of the authors for the "tragedy" of this technique is unrealistic. In addition it should be pointed out that their complete study consisted of only 25 open tests per examiner for a total of 150 tests, too small a number of tests on which to base any kind of strong inference. In their paper there is no report of what percentage of errors of false elimination and false identification respectively were found, of the duration (length) of samples used, or of how well trained, specifically in voice identification, the examiners were and who trained them. The ". . . 80 years of expertise exhibited collectively . . ." by the 6 examiners the authors employed, even with impressive credentials on spectrography, acoustic phonetics, and courses in or familiarity with voice identification, do not guarantee that they possess a training comparable with the two years of apprenticeship (at least) in dealing with practical, case-related situations that a professional examiner must have prior to taking a qualifying examination on voice identification by aural and spectrographic examination of speech samples. The authors also dismissed the contribution of aural examination in practical cases, arguing that ". . . whether it is true that by aural means individuals often can be identified with a high degree of accuracy when the speech of the talker is very well known to the listener, individuals who do not know the talkers do not tend to make accurate matches . . ." (Hollien and McGlone, 1976). To back this point they quoted the experiment by McGehee (1937). It should be brought to the attention of the reader that this statement is correct as far as the long-term memory aural examination is concerned. Because in the technique Drs. Hollien and McGlone oppose ("voiceprint") aural examinations are conducted through the short-term memory process, their statement is not applicable. Furthermore, the authors indicated that this experiment "together with a large number of others" (Endress,

Bambach, and Flosser, 1971; Hazen, 1973; Stevens et al., 1968; Young and Campbell, 1967; and 3 others) "argue against the use of this technique" (1976).

Houlihan (1977) performed an experiment searching for effects of disguise on talker identification by speech spectrograms. She used 9 female and 5 male talkers who recorded a short sentence three times in five different conditions (undisguised, lower pitch, falsetto, whispered, and muffled). With the contemporary spectrograms yielded by these recordings, closed trials of voice identification were prepared for examination by 21 examiners who received a short training prior to starting the experiment. In each trial the "unknown" voice spectrogram, prepared with the undisguised voice of each talker, had to be matched against all other talkers of the same sex, in all voice conditions. Examiners were forced to reach positive identifications or eliminations in each case. Results ranged from 100% correct decisions for undisguised voices to 5% for whispered speech.

The same author performed a second experiment using the same type of disguised voices, but including 8 male and 8 female talkers. Design of this second experiment was essentially the same as the first experiment. Results were also comparable.

These experiments suggest that examiners with little training can perform efficiently in voice identification tests using contemporary spectrograms in closed trials, but rates of error increase greatly with disguised voices if they are forced to always give a positive decision. In practical situations, because the examiner is allowed to give no-opinion decisions, the situation changes radically.

Disguising might increase the percentages of no-opinion decisions or errors of false elimination; however, mimicking a given voice could present a real danger of a costly false identification. This is especially true when the imitation is a very good one and the methods of voice identification used are not sensitive to this circumstance or the examiner is not properly trained. Hall (1976) produced a study using the mimicked voices of several personalities as made by the well-known impersonator Rich Little. Tests prepared by Hall were of the match/no-match discrimination type. The method of examination used was aural, by the short-term memory. Examiners employed in this experiment were undergraduate students with no training in this type of task. Errors of false identification, i.e., stating that the voice of Mr. Little belonged to the mimicked personality when this was not true, reached up to 20% for quiet recordings and up to 70% for recordings with noise interference. Spectrograms of the real and mimicked voices uttering the same words were also prepared. These spectrograms showed significant differences, making it easy for a professional examiner to decide they were originated by different persons. Also relevant to this matter are the experiment by Endress, Bambach, and Flosser (1971), the paper by Kersta (1962b), and the report by Gray and Kopp (1944).

Reich, Moll, and Curtis (1976) presented a study on the effects of selected vocal disguises on spectrographic talker identification. They employed 40 male talkers who were recorded twice, in sessions two weeks apart. Different sentences randomly including nine clue words were spoken in six different modes: normal speech, "old age," hoarse, hypernasal, slow rate, and a "freestyle" disguise. With spectrograms prepared from these recorded materials, open trials of voice identification were assembled, including 15 known undisguised voices to be compared with one unknown voice that could be in any of the six different modes of recording. A total of 15 trials were prepared in this manner, of which 11 were match and 4 were no-match open trials. Clue words were physically excerpted from the random text spectrograms. Four examiners received approximately 50 hours of training, including lectures and practical tests, prior to starting the experiment. These examiners were allowed to express their confidence in their own judgment using a five-point scale; however, they were not allowed to make no-opinion decisions.

Results indicated much larger percentages of correct identifications when unknown and known undisguised voices were compared than when an undisguised known voice was compared with unknown voices disguised in any mode. The difference reached a maximum of about a 40% for the "freestyle" disguised mode. Also, there was about a 15% difference in correct identifications on the same tasks as produced by different examiners.

The authors obtained a mean percentage of correct identifications of 56.67%. The 43.33% errors included false identifications and false eliminations for undisguised voices; however, the authors failed to report what the respective percentages were. There is a crucial difference between these two types of errors that cannot be logically added together. The authors compared this figure with the "approximately 80% mean of correct identifications from the Tosi et al. (1972) data for similar but not identical experimental conditions.'' Reich, Moll, and Curtis indicated several good reasons for this difference but they failed to perceive the principal one, in the opinion of the author, the physical excerption of the clue words from the random text spectrograms, which is contrary to the Tosi et al. procedure. Excerpting words from a continuous spectrogram might destroy transients, which are important clues for voice identification. In addition, determining exact boundaries for each word physically excerpted from an ongoing text on a spectrogram is difficult and sometimes impossible.

As a laboratory study, the Reich, Moll, and Curtis experiment is useful to show quantitatively the differences between spectrographic identifications of undisguised and disguised voices. However, results from this experiment can hardly be extrapolated to practical situations due to several factors: unknown and known samples used by professional examiners are of the same context and are longer than the ones utilized in this study, clue words are not physically excerpted from the spectrograms, and the professional examiner, in addition to having at least 2 years of practical training, is entitled to a no-opinion decision when he does not feel confident enough to render a positive decision.

Variability Produced by the Transmitting and Recording Channels

For this discussion it will be assumed that the voice samples (both the criminal's and defendant's voices) are obtained through a telephone line and consequently are tape recorded. In addition to the noise that can exist at any stage of the transmitting and recording channels (masking to a larger or smaller degree the voice samples), the environment in which the talker is using the telephone provides some particular resonances to the speech wave. As a result of the particular acoustics of the room in which the talker is speaking into a telephone receiver, some bands of frequency will be amplified, some others will be damped. If the defendant were to have a sample of his speech recorded within the same room, the interaction of this type of resonance might have no major effect on the correctness of the identification or elimination. This is especially true in any case where both the unknown and the known samples are equally affected by the same type of resonances. However, because very often in legal cases the location of the telephone used by the criminal caller is not known, resonances might differ markedly from those encountered in the room where the defendant was producing his voice samples. This factor should be given the proper consideration by the examiners; however, in the opinion of the author, the effect of these resonances is not important in most cases.

What might produce more significant effects is the resonance or response curve of the telephone line utilized. Most telephone lines restrict the passing range of frequencies, normally to from 150 to 4,000 Hz; in addition, the resonances and response curves of the lines amplify and attenuate respectively some bands of frequencies within that range. The pick-up device, or method of connecting the receiving telephone to the tape recorder, and the tape recorder itself, can also introduce distortions to both the unknown and the defendant's samples. In every case the so-called response curve of each of the transmitting and recording elements utilized should be obtained to have information on this type of distortion.

The response curve of an element is a graph in which intensity outputs are plotted as a function of frequencies; to plot the response curve the input to the testing device must be pure tones (sinusoidal waves) of constant intensity and, of course, variable frequency (Figure 2.14). Knowledge of these response curves might allow examiners to cancel their distortional effects on the voice samples. However, in many cases this type of peculiar frequency response interaction could introduce confusion. For instance, in the project of semiautomatic voice identification by the Aerospace Corporation (1977) the system worked perfectly well for samples of voices recorded directly but failed for voices recorded through the telephone.

Bunge[4] suggested a procedure to eliminate the influence of telephone response curve. The first step is to record samples from different speakers directly into a tape recorder, segmenting short samples of steady portions (vowels) from these samples, and producing a Fourier transform. The next step consists of computing the variance of amplitude within each frequency for all similar phonetic samples from the subjects. This variance is compared with a similar parameter from analogous segments from the unknown telephone recording. Such a ratio might be used to cancel the interaction of the telephone line, providing that it is a linear transfer function. This linearity might be hindered by carbon microphones utilized by the telephone companies.

---

[4] Dr. Ernest Bunge, Research Director of the Bundeskriminalamt (W. Germany), during a visit to the Michigan State University Institute of Voice Identification, made this personal communication to the author.

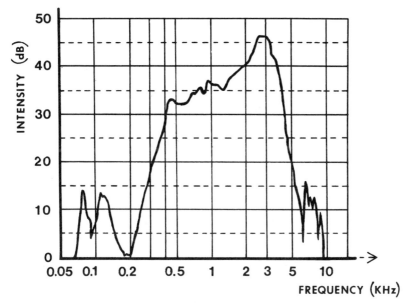

Figure 2.14. Response curve of a transmitting and recording system, including a commercial telephone line and a magnetic pick-up attached at the receiver end of the line.

Another procedure that might lead to elimination of perturbing telephone influence could consist of including a "standard" burst sound at the beginning of every telephone communication. Because the real spectrum of such a "standard" sound would be known, the transfer function of the telephone line could then be easily computed.

The defendant's voice samples should be recorded using the same type of tape recorder and telephone line as used to obtain the criminal's voice recordings, when these types are known. In cases where an informer has obtained the criminal's voice samples, this information is available. When the criminal has called a victim at his house or office, or has made calls to a police headquarters, factory, etc., there is also a partial knowledge of the utilized channels. Samples from the defendant's voice should be obtained through similar channels.

Summary

Organic and learned differences are the sources of intertalker variability. Additional variability is introduced by environmental reverberations, noise, and distortions from the transmission and re-cording systems. Considering all these sources of variability, there is little hope of ever developing a method, or rather a clustering of methods, that could provide a positive talker identification or elim-ination in 100% of all cases examined, within a legally acceptable rate of error. In many cases, whether the methods used are objective or subjective, the outcome of the examination has to be *no decision one way or the other* (or no probability of identification or elimi-nation) if the examiner, regardless of the method used, is very well trained, unbiased, and proceeding within strict rules of professional integrity.

To demand that a system of voice identification be resistant to disguise, noise, or other distortions for practical use is unrealistic and unfair. No system of identification is resistant to drastic dis-tortions, including fingerprinting, handwriting analysis, etc.

On the other hand, most of the variabilities discussed could increase the percentage of no-opinion decisions, or at the worst the percentage of errors of false elimination, rather than the errors of false identification. Indeed, most of these distortions tend to in-crease the intraspeaker differences, which only can lead toward false elimination rather than toward false identification. This type of error is not so costly for our system of justice as the error of false identification is.

chapter 3
METHODS OF VOICE IDENTIFICATION AND ELIMINATION

OVERVIEW OF METHODS OF
VOICE IDENTIFICATION AND ELIMINATION

This section is not intended to produce an exhaustive review of all experiments done on voice identification. Only a sample of them is discussed here in order to give the reader a brief, although reasonable, account of available experimental data on the topic. Persons interested in further pursuing this particular aspect might consult other sources, such as "Speaker Recognition" by Bricker and Pruzansky (1976).

On the other hand, the reader should be warned that most of the laboratory experiments on voice identification performed to date share one common characteristic—their results are very hard to compare because experimental conditions among them differ widely and data were reported differently.[1] Also, extrapolations from laboratory experiments to practical, case-related situations could become very controversial, because of differences of opinions concerning the validity of such extrapolations.

A classification of methods of voice identification and elimination was presented in Chapter 1. The reader should recall the fact that the different methods are not exclusive; that is, two or more of them might be used simultaneously in practical cases. Also, it should be noted that until recently only subjective methods were used for forensic applications, either aural methods or the combi-

---

[1] In many experiments related to voice identification, especially by visual examination of spectrograms, percentage errors of false elimination were not reported—only percentage of correct identification was reported (Hollien and McGlone, 1976; Reich, Moll, and Curtis, 1976). Because there is a crucial difference in the implications of these two types of errors, results from these experiments are difficult to interpret properly.

nation of aural and spectrographic examination of speech samples, popularly and wrongly called "voiceprinting." It is probable that in the future semiautomatic and automatic methods will also be introduced in courts of law.

SUBJECTIVE METHODS OF
TALKER IDENTIFICATION AND ELIMINATION

Aural examinations of recorded voices and visual examinations of speech spectrograms are considered subjective methods of talker identification, each within a different category of subjectivity. A summary of available experimental data on these methods is presented in the next two sections.

Aural Examination of Voices

A listener may use the long-term memory process or the short-term memory process to identify or eliminate an unknown talker as being the same as a particular known one. These two memory processes are used according to the particular situation as follows:

The long-term memory process is utilized when the voice to be identified is one familiar to the listener.

The short-term memory process is used when the unknown and known voices to be compared are not familiar to the examiner but they are continually and permanently available through magnetic tape recordings.

The long-term memory process can be used by any witness in a court of law. The short-term memory process demands the assistance of an expert witness.

The success of aural recognition based on long-term memory depends on the remembrance or the familiarity of the listener with the known voice, the time elapsed since it was last heard by the listener, the homogeneity of the talkers involved, and the discriminating ability of the listener. The voice sample duration is apparently not critical after 1 sec of continuous speech, in normal circumstances. If a transmission or recording system is used to obtain known talkers' voice samples, distortions introduced by such a system may increase the percentage of errors. Filtering below 500 Hz and above 3,000 Hz seems to have no significant influence on the results of tests. This information is important because most voice evidence is obtained through the telephone line, which usually filters harmonics of speech below 150 Hz and above 4,000 Hz. Attempts of the talkers to disguise their voices, or even to use whispered speech, may decrease the correct identification percentage by this method (Pollack, Pickett, and Sumby, 1954).

The first significant experiment done in the area of aural examination, using the long-term memory process, was performed by McGehee (1937, 1944). She used a total of 31 male and 18 female talkers, reading a paragraph of 56 words. Apparently, these talkers belonged to a phonetically homogeneous group, all university graduate students. A total of 740 undergraduate students with no special training were employed as listeners in this experiment, in which live voices (no recordings) were used exclusively. Listeners were divided into 15 panels, each panel participating in at least two sessions. During the first session they listened to a talker behind a screen reading a paragraph. During the second session, 5 talkers, including the one from the first session, read the same paragraph. Each listener had to indicate who among these 5 talkers was the one they had heard previously. The second listening session was spaced somewhere from one day to five months after the first one, differing for each particular panel of listeners. The average percentage of correct identification varied from 83% to 13%, according to the time elapsed; the higher percentage corresponds to a one-day lapse, and the lower percentage corresponds to a five-month lapse between first and second listening sessions.

McGehee also investigated the effects of disguising the voice by changing the pitch, which drastically reduced the percentage of correct identifications. Other findings of this early study were that male and female voices are equally identifiable and that increasing the number of known talkers reduces the percentage of correct identification. It should be noted that all tests of identification used in this experiment were the closed type using long-term memory, and that no recordings were employed.

Pollack, Pickett, and Sumby (1954) also performed an experiment on aural recognition based on the long-term memory. All 16 talkers used in this experiment were familiar to the listeners who performed the "speaker-naming tests" for groups varying from 2 to 8 talkers. Speech samples used in this experiment were tape-recorded.

The authors investigated the effect of three variables on the percentage of correct identifications—duration of the speech sample, filtering, and whispering. Their findings are summarized as follows:

Using normal speech samples that are longer than 1 sec does not significantly improve the percentage of correct identification, which reached a figure close to 95% for this interval of time.

Whispered speech reduces to approximately 30% the percentage of correct identifications, with other conditions constant.

Whispered speech samples should have a duration of at least 3 sec to obtain the same percentage of correct identification as obtained with normal speech.

For low-pass and high-pass filtering, the authors concluded that "over a rather wide frequency range, identification performance is resistant to selective frequency of this type." However, filtering above 500 Hz and below 2,000 Hz decreased the percentage of correct identification.

In this experiment, the authors used a phonetically balanced list of monosyllabic words from the Harvard Psychoacoustic Laboratory.

Bricker and Pruzansky (1966) studied the effects of stimulus content and duration on aural voice identification. They used 16 examiners and 10 talkers with whom the examiners were familiar. The talkers recorded many different materials using high fidelity equipment. The examiners listened to these voices through a loudspeaker. The best examiner was able to obtain 100% correct identification when listening to sentences with a mean duration of 2.4 sec containing about 15 phonemes. The worst examiner for the same tests obtained 92% correct responses. These percentages dropped to 56% correct for samples with a duration of 0.12 sec containing only one phoneme. The authors found a significant interaction between particular phonemes and talkers for these brief excerpted phonetic materials. They also ran tests based on short-term memory, including 2 known subjects, A and B, to be compared with one unknown subject X. For these tests the listeners were not familiar with the talkers. Average results of correct identification in these closed tests using short-term memory reached the 75% level.

Coleman (1973) used 2 male and 10 female talkers and 28 listeners to perform a study of voice identification using short-term memory and match/no-match discrimination tests. The influence of the speaker's glottal source was eliminated by using an artificial larynx vibrating at a fundamental frequency of 85 Hz to record speech samples for all talkers. Samples consisted of a 5-sec segment of ongoing speech. The average percentage of correct identification was 90% for listeners with no special training who were forced to give a positive decision in each trial. Coleman concluded logically that the resonances of the vocal tract are the clues for voice identification rather than the glottal characteristics of the talker, including pitch.

Some authors took a different approach to studying aural identifcation, trying to determine significant perceptual attributes of talkers' voices in order to create reliable classification scales. These scales might help an examiner to perform aural discriminations on a systematic and consistent basis. A classic study of this type was undertaken by Voiers (1964), who was able to isolate four significant perceptual scales—clarity, roughness, magnitude, and animation—to use as a means to discriminate among speakers. Holmgren (1967) found that pitch, intensity, quality, and speech rate scales helped to better classify the uniqueness of each particular voice. However, in practical cases it was verified that the same set of numbers from the four scales given to one voice might also correspond to other different voices. Therefore, perceptual scales should be considered only as a helping device for talker identification or elimination.

One of the few studies in aural examination using both open and closed trials with the short-term memory process was performed by Stevens et al. (1968). In this study the authors attempted to compare results obtained from aural examination and from visual examination of spectrograms, using the same materials and the same examiners. They employed 24 talkers who were highly homogeneous from the point of view of perceptual attributes of speech. All of these talkers recorded a reading list of nine isolated words and two short sentences, all repeated 10 times. They recorded these materials twice, one week apart. These materials were dubbed into magnetic tape loops of 4.5 sec duration, each loop containing two utterances of the same words or one utterance of a short sentence. Spectrograms of these materials were also subsequently prepared. Six examiners performed open and closed tests of talker identification and elimination with these materials, using aural and visual examinations separately. They did not receive training for either of the two methods; however, they were selected on the basis of their abilities to become aurally familiar with a group of six previously unfamiliar voices. No tests on their ability to match spectrograms were reported.

All tests in this experiment, both open and closed types, included 1 unknown and 8 known talkers. The examiners could listen to the nine tape loops representing these talkers, switching as necessary among nine tape recorder playback channels.

In all cases the percentages of correct responses were significantly higher for aural examination than for visual examination. For the closed tests mean errors of false identification yielded by aural examination ranged from 18% to 6%. Mean errors of false identification yielded by visual examination of spectrograms of the same materials ranged from 28% to 21%. The lower percentages correspond to later tests when some learning effect had obviously interacted with the results. For the open tests results were as follows: aural method, 8% to 6% error of false identification and 12% to 8% error of false elimination; visual method, 47% to 31% error of false identification and 20% to 10% error of false elimination.

This author feels that these percentages were biased because the examiners had normal hearing and were accustomed to discriminating voices aurally from the early stages of life, but they were *not* familiar with matching spectrograms—at least they had had no special training in the use of spectrograms for voice identification. Furthermore, the examiners in this study were selected on the basis of their aural ability, but their ability to match spectrographic patterns was not tested. Also, the lengths of the samples used were inadequate for spectrographic recognition. In a letter to prosecutor P. Lindhom of St. Paul, Minnesota (28 January 1971), Dr. Stevens acknowledged that these factors might be the reason for the high percentage of errors in visual examination produced in his experiment.

Some valuable conclusions from this study were that: 1) some talkers are more difficult to identify than others even when the talker population tested is homogeneous from the point of view of the perceptual attributes; 2) there are large differences in the ability to identify a talker by listening to his front vowels rather than to his back vowels; 3) longer utterances increase the probability of correct identifications using visual spectrographic examination.

In sum, aural examination of voices is the most familiar and natural system of speaker identification and elimination. It is accepted by any court of law at face value. The expected percentage of error for open tests, using the short-term memory process (i.e., listening through recordings to the known and unknown voices), has not been accurately determined by experimentation. It might be as large as 20%, according to particular circumstances, especially if the examiner is forced to reach a positive decision in all tests instead of alternatively selecting probabilities or being allowed to choose a no-opinion answer. Distortions, masking noise, and disguise of the voice can increase the percentages of expected errors or no-opinion decisions. Through consideration of the available experimentation, it can be concluded that some listeners perform better than others on tasks of talker identification and elimination by aural methods. There is no available laboratory data on whether or not the critical listening ability can be improved by proper training, that is, by constant practice and concentration. However, this author is convinced that this is true. This belief is based on his evaluation of performance of voice identification trainees at the Michigan State University. Also, laboratory data show that some groups of talkers yield more errors than others, keeping all other conditions equal.

As previously stated, the short-term memory technique has introduced the expert witness in aural methods of voice identification in place of the witness called to testify by using the long-term memory alternative. Expert witnesses using the short-term memory method by itself or in combination with other methods are either voice identification practitioners or speech scientists who produce laboratory examinations of the unknown and known voices prior to presentation in a court of law. Perceptual characteristics of the unknown and known voices, such as quality, rhythm, melody pattern, pitch, rate, and respiratory group, are evaluated in the laboratory in order to produce a subjective opinion as to whether or not they belong to the same talker.

At the Institute of Voice Identification of the Michigan State University these known talker/unknown talker evaluations are done by using loop cartridges played back simultaneously through a pair of tape recorders connected to a two-channel amplifier. A fast manipulation of a switch allows the examiner to listen at will to either voice, repeating continuously the same sentence recorded in any of the four 1.5 min duration loops of each cartridge. In this author's opinion this method presents advantages over the use of open reel tapes for the same purpose.

The author also believes that in spite of the modern trend to investigate automatic methods, continuing research on aural examination is worthwhile. Experimental designs on this method should include open and discrimination match/no-match tests, and use of low quality recording systems, telephone line transmission, and background noise to approximate as closely as possible practical, case-related situations.

Visual Examination of Speech Spectrograms

As was discussed in the section on "Acoustics" in Chapter 2, acoustic or speech spectrography consists of a display of the main parameters of a speech wave: time, frequencies, and power or intensity within each range of frequencies. Such a display presents successive Fourier short-term spectra of the temporally variable speech signal.

This operation was first performed for sustained vowels early in this century using mechanical spectrographs such as the Henrici analyzer. Black (1937) was able to produce this type of tridimensional spectra of the same vowel as spoken by different talkers. These early studies showed patently the intertalker variability, as disclosed by the difference in spectra of the same phonemes when uttered by different persons.

In 1941, an electromechanical acoustic spectrograph project led by Dr. Ralph Potter (Potter, Kopp, and Green, 1947) was started at the Bell Telephone Laboratories. The machine was developed with the primary purpose of helping the military during the war. Only when World War II was over did the spectrograph become available to speech scientists.

The input to the spectrograph is a tape-recorded speech sample limited to loop segments 2.4 sec long. Of course, successive samples of this duration can be processed to complete any desired total sample length. The output consists of a graphic display (spectrogram) of frequency/intensity of sound over time for the sample analyzed. The display is obtained on a special paper placed on a rotating drum. Standard spectrographic paper size is 32 cm by 14.3 cm.

On the spectrogram, frequencies are plotted on the vertical axis, time on the horizontal axis, and relative intensities are portrayed by the different degrees of darkness of the patterns produced (on bar spectrograms). In the commercially available spectrographs (Figure 3.1), there are several options for setting the ranges of sound frequencies for analysis (60 to 4,000 Hz or 60 to 7,000 Hz, etc.), using logarithmic or linear scales. Each 2.4-sec speech segment to be analyzed is played back by a rotating electromagnetic head that scans a loop from the magnetic tape where the sample is recorded. The electrical output of the playback head is analyzed by a scanning

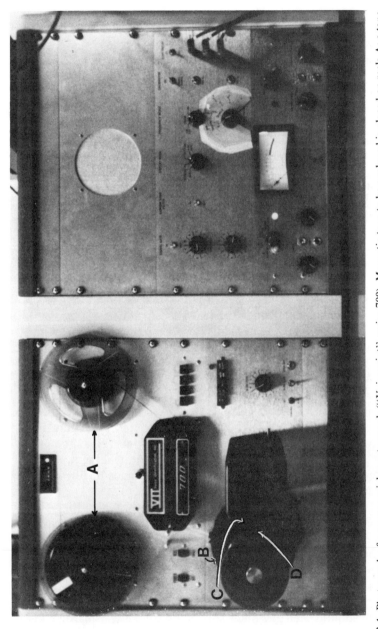

Figure 3.1. Photograph of a commercial spectrograph ("Voiceprint" series 700). Magnetic tape to be analyzed is placed on reels A; a tape loop including a 2.4 sec speech is selected at drum B, which contains the rotating playback head; spectrographic paper is placed on rotating drum C (synchronized with playback head B); stylus D scans rotating paper from bottom to top, producing the spectrogram.

filter through the range of frequencies selected. The bandwidth of the analyzing scanning filter can be set at 45 or 300 Hz. If the narrowband scanning filter (45 Hz) is selected, the actual Fourier harmonics of the input speech sample are displayed on the spectrogram. If the broadband scanning filter (300 Hz) is utilized, formants of vowels or higher power bands of consonants, rather than the individual harmonics, appear on the spectrogram. Both types of displays are called bar spectrograms. Instantaneous outputs of the scanning filter are transferred to a stylus that slides along the width of a rotating drum holding the spectrographic paper; this spectrographic paper drum rotates synchronically with the loop playback head. The spectrographic paper is electrically burned according to the speech intensity at each point of the time/frequency display. It is also possible to obtain contour spectrograms with these devices. In the contour spectrograms relative intensities are portrayed by isobaric lines spaced 6 dB from each other.

In sum, it can be stated that the operation of the spectrograph consists essentially of displaying a continuous short-term Fourier analysis of the speech sample, at each instant of time, on a special sensitive paper ("Teledeltos" paper).

Because the relative intensity of each harmonic or each formant is portrayed by the different degrees of darkness of the patterns produced, and the intensity range of the speech formants can be as large as 40 dB, a compressor circuit in the machine can increase the intensity of the input signal in proportion (at different rates) to the scanned range of frequencies. One preferred rate is 12 dB per octave of intensity increase. The reason for this procedure is to compensate for the reduced dynamic range of the Teledeltos paper (about 10 dB) where the spectrogram is printed, making it possible to record on the paper the weak, higher harmonics or formants of the speech signal.

The original spectrograph design, marketed by Kay Elemetrics (Pine Brook, N.J.) was improved in 1966 by Anthony Presti, an engineer at the Bell Telephone Laboratories, who later joined the Voiceprint Laboratories, Inc. (N.J.) to market his new improved spectrograph under the brand name "Voiceprint" (Presti, 1966). He also introduced the feature of isobaric contour display in the instrument.

The sound spectrograph or sonograph can be considered a kind of universal instrument for researching and teaching acoustics in general or speech sound in particular. In addition, it was used for practical applications such as improving the speech of deaf people. However, in 1944, Gray and Kopp found that spectrograms could be applied to the identification of speakers because the spectrograms not only portray the phonetic features of speech but talker-dependent features as well. This potential use had an important war application at that time. United States intelligence had knowledge that each German division always used the same radio operator for communications. Through goniometry the direction of German army transmissions could be easily obtained. Therefore, if the voice of a particular radio operator could be identified, evaluation of successive radio transmissions might have disclosed the movements of each German division. Because this information was valuable to the U.S., and it would depend on a reliable method of voice identification, Drs. Gray and Kopp became very enthusiastic about developing this project. They wrote a report (Gray and Kopp, 1944) describing their experiences in this field and suggesting means to put this method into practical use, how to train examiners to identify talkers, etc. They coined the word "voiceprinting" to designate the application of speech spectrograms to voice identification. On page 1 of this report, Gray and Kopp wrote:

> Much more simple and quantitative than the aural scheme is a technique based upon the Sound Spectrograph, an instrument which makes permanent patterns of speech that can be examined visually in the way fingerprints or handwriting can be examined and can be filed as reference samples.

Also, they were concerned with attempts at disguising the voice:

> . . . there might be occasional cases where voice alteration is attempted to imitate some important individual and some consideration of its effects, therefore, is in order. The voice may be altered either by impersonation or disguise. Figs. 6A, B, C and D show the words "Voice Print Identification" spoken in a natural voice by one individual and imitated as closely as possible by another individual who is an expert in phonetics. It was difficult to distinguish between these two samples by ear but a cursory examination of the voice prints reveals detectable differences in these records.

Drs. Gray and Kopp concluded their report with the following paragraph:

> Voice print identification seems to offer the possibility of a useful radio intercept feature and one that could be put into use without extensive training or elaborate equipment. As a study of combat conditions in the European and Pacific theaters indicates a need for such

identification, it is suggested that a trial voice identification group be established to carry on the work under actual or simulated field conditions to test the conclusions of this laboratory work.

To the best knowledge of this author, such a test was not completed, probably due to the problem of obtaining recordings and to the end of the war. The tape recorder, or rather the wire recorder, was not practically developed or extensively used at that time. The common available means of recording speech samples was the phonographic disc; it was considered inconvenient for the purpose of obtaining voice evidence samples from practical situations.

During the early 1960s, Mr. Lawrence Kersta, a staff member of the Bell Telephone Laboratories, reexamined the "voiceprint" method at the request of a law enforcement group that wanted to use evidence obtained through tape-recorded telephone conversations.

He performed laboratory experiments using spectrograms from five clue words spoken in isolation by an unspecified population (Kersta, 1962a). All the tests were of the closed type, using contemporary spectrograms, that is, spectrograms produced from talker samples obtained during the same recording session. The maximum number of known talkers in each trial of identification was 12. The examiners were requested to render a positive decision in all cases as to which of the known talkers was the same as the "unknown" one. These examiners were a group of high school girls trained by Kersta for one week prior to the starting of the experiment. Examiners worked in pairs. The percentage of correct identifications in these experiments was better than 99%. In the Kersta papers there was no report of significant differences among examiners' performances. Homogeneity and number of talkers utilized were not discussed. Other experiments that Kersta performed, such as sorting spectrograms in order to form groups including the same talker, also showed a high percentage of correct responses.

Kersta became absolutely convinced of the "infallibility" of the spectrograms for identification purposes and presented a paper to the November 1962 meeting of the Acoustical Society of America in which he compared the reliability of this method with that of fingerprints (Kersta, 1962b).

In 1966, Kersta retired from Bell Telephone Laboratories and established his own company, Voiceprint Laboratories, Inc., with the goal of producing spectrographic instruments on a commercial basis. He also offered his professional services to identify persons through their voices and to train police officers as speech spectrogram examiners.

The scientific community soon voiced its opposition to Kersta's claims. Some experiments that contradicted the extremely high success percentages reported by Kersta were produced by several speech scientists. One of the most adamant opponents of Kersta at that time was Dr. Peter Ladefoged, who published a paper (Ladefoged and Vanderslice, 1967) contradicting the statements of Kersta. Further information on this controversy may be found in the section on "Legality of Voice Identification before December 1970" in Chapter 5.

Young and Campbell (1967) published a study dealing with closed tests or talker identification by visual examination of spectrograms. Five talkers uttering two words were used as known talkers in each trial. Young and Campbell used 10 examiners who received a maximum of 2.5 hr of training before the beginning of the experiment. During this training phase, using 1 clue word ("you" or "it") spoken in isolation, the identification success reached a mean of 78.4%. During the experimental tasks, spectrograms of the same two words ("you," "it") were used, but this time they were excerpted from a sentence rather than produced in isolation. The percentage of success decreased to a mean of 37.3%. Young and Campbell attribute these differences to the shorter stimulus represented by the excerpted words, as compared with the longer stimulus of the words uttered in isolation, and to the coarticulation factors. They recognized, however, that the different experimental approach they took, as compared with that of Kersta, the difference in training of examiners, and possibly differences in population homogeneity could have accounted for the different score percentages obtained in the two experiments.

Stevens et al. (1968) performed another experiment using aural examination and visual examination of spectrograms separately. A discussion of and results from this experiment were presented in the previous section on "Aural Examination of Voices."

In a published thesis, Hazen (1973) reported an experiment performed to determine the effects of context on talker identification. He used 5 clue words physically excerpted from spectrograms obtained from spontaneous talkers' speech and seven team panels, each composed of 2 examiners who received a few sessions of training before the starting of the experiment. There were different types of tasks to be performed, including absolute identification or elimination of 1 unknown talker among 50 known ones. Hazen forced the examiners to reach a positive decision in all of the 40 tests performed by each panel. The range of errors varied from 0% to 83.33% according to the type of error, the task, and the panel. The error was always larger when comparing excerpted words from different speech contexts than when words taken from the same speech context were compared. This is illustrated in Hazen's Table VI by the fact that panel 4 produced 0% errors of false identification and 83% errors of false elimination. Panel 1 doing exactly the same the tests produced 56% errors of false identification and 33% errors of false elimination. From these results Hazen concluded that voice identification using spectrograms should not be utilized "until sufficient and consistent data are gathered to establish accurately the limits of this technique" (1973).

Certainly, this would be a most reasonable conclusion if speech spectrograms of 5 clue words physically excerpted from different texts were used as the sole means of identification in practical cases, by examiners with no experience who were forced to render a positive decision in 100% of the cases examined. It should be pointed out that Hazen's idea of using words from spontaneous speech as opposed to words from readings was an excellent one, because in practical cases the unknown person indeed uses spontaneous speech. However, to physically excerpt these words from continuous speech spectrograms was not a commendable procedure because it is almost impossible to target the boundaries of a word within a spectrogram. Furthermore, transient patterns are talker-dependent features, and they become lost with this procedure. In addition, only 40 trials of absolute identification or elimination per panel (or 280 trials in total) do not constitute an impressive amount of statistical data to solidly substantiate any recommendation.

The merit of Hazen's study is in having reiterated what should not be done with spectrograms—physically excerpt spectrographic patterns of a given word from an ongoing text, and use random contexts for matching techniques. Also, the fact that one panel (panel 4) produced 0% errors of false identification in open tests, using only 5 clue words distorted by coarticulation and not being allowed to give no-opinion decisions, speaks very favorably about this method. Indeed, the conclusions that can be drawn from Table VI of Hazen's paper can be expressed as follows: this experiment, even restricted in amount of data as it is, suggests that voice identification by visual examination of spectrograms can be very valid or not, depending on the examiner. Using only 5 clue words, physically excerpted from spectrograms of ongoing speech of different contexts, not being allowed to give no-opinion decisions, panel 4 produced 0% errors of false identification. However, panel 1, examining the same materials and tests, produced 56% of false identification. The errors of false identification possibly could have become no-opinion decisions if examiners had been allowed that alternative. This point should be further investigated.

The reader can observe how such opposite conclusions were derived from the same data, and is invited to draw his own conclusions from Hazen's experiment.

Smrkovski (1976) performed a study on voice identification by aural examination and visual examination of spectrograms, using the following conditions: noncontemporary speech samples from male and female talkers; examiners with different degrees of expertise; and open discrimination trials randomly arranged. Procedures recommended by the International Association of Voice Identification (see Chapter 4) were followed in this study.

The number of talkers used in this experiment was 14, 7 male and 7 female, all native speakers of the General American English dialect. Each sample consisted of a sentence comprised of 9 words. Each talker was represented by two samples separated by a lapse of 15 months. The total number of examiners was 12, divided into three groups according to expertise: 4 professional examiners approved by the International Association of Voice Identification; 4 trainees with less than two years practice; and 4 novices.

Trials were of the match/no-match discrimination type; 50% of them were match and 50% were no-match trials, randomly arranged. Each examiner was presented with 10 trials to be completed by using the combined aural and visual examination method; they were allowed to select one out of five alternative decisions for each trial— positive identification or elimination, probability of identification or elimination, and no opinion one way or the other. Results were as follows: professional examiners and trainees produced no errors of false identification or elimination; novices produced 5% error of false identification and 25% error of false elimination. Probability of identification or elimination answers were in total 15% for professionals, 40% for trainees, and 50% for novices. No-opinion decisions were 7.5% of the decisions for professionals, 2.5% for trainees, and 2.5% for novices.

This experiment, although including a total of only 120 trials,

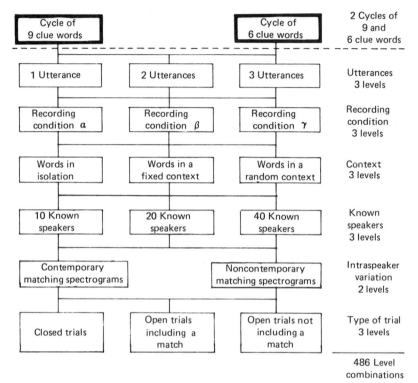

Figure 3.2. Experimental design of the Tosi et al. (1972) study of voice identification by visual examination of spectrograms. For each cycle of 9 or 6 clue words, 486 different types of trials were performed by 9 subpanels of examiners. This process was repeated four times. The total number of responses for each type of trial was 36, and the total number of responses for each cycle was 17,496.

suggests that the experience of the examiner has an important effect on the reliability of this combined aural and visual examination method of voice identification.

It should be noted that professional examiners in this experiment produced a larger percentage of no-opinion decisions than the trainees or novices; this finding supports the notion that a trained examiner is more cautious than a partially trained one.

To date, the most extensive study on voice identification and elimination by using speech spectrograms has been performed by the author and his associates (Tosi et al., 1972) at Michigan State University. This study was supported through a large grant from the United States Department of Justice;[2] it was carried out from the beginning of 1968 through December 1970. This experiment included a total of 34,992 experimental trials of identification and elimination, according to different models of an experimental design (Figure 3.2). Each test in this experiment involved the use of up to 40 "known" voices and one to three utterances of the same text in various conditions: closed and open trials, contemporary and non-contemporary spectrograms, and 9 or 6 clue words spoken in isolation, in a fixed context, and in random context. Effects of transmission channels and noise were also considered by recording the samples directly into a tape recorder or through a telephone line in a quiet or in a noisy condition. Each combination of variables determined the type of model tested. The forensic models consisted of open tests, noncontemporary spectrograms, telephone transmission, and fixed or random context, thus closely simulating practical legal cases. The total number of trials included in the forensic models was 11,664. Other models including closed tests, contemporary spectrograms, direct transmission into a tape recorder, and words spoken in isolation were represented by a total of 5,832 trials. Models including noncontemporary spectrograms were represented by 11,664 trials; additional models including open tests were represented by 5,832. These models were tested either to have a relative scale of measurement or to replicate Kersta's experiments.[3]

The tests were performed by 29 selected examiners who received practical training for one month prior to the start of the experiment. Examiners were divided into three panels according to sex and type of educational background. Each panel was further subdivided into three subpanels of one, two, and three persons (Figure 3.3). Eleven examiners were used as substitutes to replace absentees. They rotated within the subpanels and were paid by the hour.

These examiners were forced to reach a positive decision (iden-

---

[2] Dr. Herbert Oyer was very instrumental in helping to obtain funds. He also acted as the administrative director of the project.

[3] An opponent of voice identification by aural and spectrographic examination of speech samples has stated several times in a court of law that the Tosi experiment included only a certain number of tests related to forensic models. However, he changed the "actual" number on different occasions (36 one time and 12 another). Also, a simple reading of the methods of the experiment will show what the actual number is. A judge commented that "this witness cannot keep his numbers straight between 5 and 20,000."

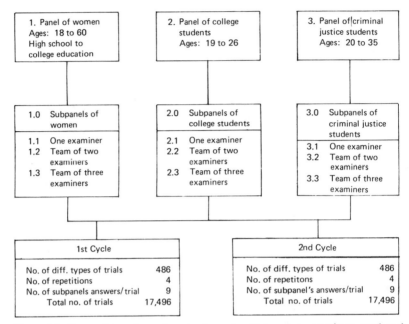

Figure 3.3. Composition of panels and subpanels of laboratory examiners employed in the Tosi et al. (1972) study. These laboratory examiners received one month of practical training prior to the start of the experiment. (Note: for the 2nd cycle the subpanels of three members were replaced by subpanels of two members.)

tification or elimination) in each test, taking an average time of 15 minutes. Their decisions were based solely on examination of spectrograms; aural examination was discarded from this experiment. The examiners rated their self-confidence in their judgments on a 4-point scale: 1 and 2, almost and fairly uncertain, respectively; 3 and 4, fairly and almost certain, respectively.

The percentage of errors of false identification obtained from the forensic models of the experimental design (open tests, noncontemporary spectrograms, and continuous speech) tested in this experiment was approximately 6.4%. The percentage of errors of false elimination from the same models was approximately 12.7%. Kersta's models (closed tests, contemporary spectrograms, words spoken in isolation) were also tested in this experiment and yielded a percentage of errors of less than 1%.

The total number of uncertain and certain ratings of answers by the examiners was computed in order to determine the possible error percentages that would have been obtained if the examiners had not been forced to reach a positive conclusion in 100% of the tests. It was determined by computer calculation that in 74% of the tests the examiners graded their decisions as "certain" (either 4, almost, or 3, fairly certain). Computer calculations then yielded 2.4% false identification errors and 4.18% false elimination errors for the forensic models whose results were judged as "certain" by the examiners.

These results should be considered only as a kind of numbers guide when trying to apply them to practical, case-related situations, due to the different conditions found within the laboratory and the "field" (the legal system). Some factors encountered in actual cases might have a negative influence and others might have a positive influence on the probability of error. Laboratory talkers' speech and spectrograms are in general better than spontaneous speech spectrograms from the unknown criminal recorded during the commission of a crime, which tends to increase errors of elimination or no-opinion decisions in legal cases. But the experience and responsibility of a professional examiner, together with his ability to choose alternative decisions after examinations, including "no opinion one way or the other", his aural comparison of the samples, and his freedom to take all necessary time to complete the examination, as compared with the restrictions of the laboratory examiner (in our experiment, the examiners were students with little training and without the resource of making a no-opinion decision in case of doubt), might have a decisive weight in decreasing the percentage of errors.

With the purpose of actually testing the effects of the differences between laboratory conditions and practical conditions that might be encountered by a professional examiner, at the same time that the laboratory study was being conducted by Tosi a field study was completed at the Crime Laboratory of the Michigan State Police by Lt. Ernest Nash (Tosi et al., 1972). Lt. Nash was previously trained for two years in voice identification by speech spectrograms. The field study included 673 voice samples from people involved in actual criminal investigations. A positive identification was obtained in only approximately 15% of the cases; the correctness of these decisions was later corroborated in many instances by evidence other than the voices. In about 50% of the cases studied a no-opinion answer was given by the examiner. This field study was conducted by using concurrently both aural short-term memory examination of recordings and visual examination of spectrograms. None of these cases was subsequently taken to court, in keeping with the just experimental goals of the study.

Combined Aural and Visual Examination

After evaluation of laboratory conditions and "field" conditions from the Tosi et al. and Nash studies, the following conclusion was reached: a combined method of aural and visual examination of speech samples can be used in the investigation of a crime providing that the following standards are maintained:

1. The examiner must be a qualified professional trained in phonetics and speech sciences. A two-year apprenticeship in field work should be required along with academic training before a voice examiner can be qualified professionally.
2. The professional examiner must abstain from offering any positive conclusion when he has the least doubt on the exactness of such a conclusion. Because this method is essentially subjective and relies heavily on the expertise of the examiner, prudence should be the cardinal principle that guides the examiner's decisions. The examiner should select among the following alternative decisions after completing the examination:
   a) Positive identification (a high degree of confidence that the unknown voice is the same as a known one)
   b) Probability of identification
   c) Positive elimination (a high degree of confidence that the unknown voice is different from the known ones)
   d) Probability of elimination
   e) No opinion one way or the other
3. The examiner must be entitled to spend as much time and to demand as many voice samples of good quality as he deems necessary for reaching a positive conclusion. Otherwise, he should select alternative decisions, such as probability of identification or elimination or simply no opinion one way or the other.
4. The samples of the defendant's voice should include the same contextual materials as found in the unknown voice.

In keeping with these standards, the Michigan State Police decided to employ this combined aural and visual method of talker identification or elimination starting in December 1970; the opinion of several responsible speech scientists was that these standards would tend to decrease the laboratory error percentages (Black et al., 1973).[4] Other persons maintained the contrary (Bolt et al., 1973). Very shortly after these studies, the International Association of Voice Identification, a nonprofit organization, was founded with the purpose of testing examiners, providing standards and a code of ethics, and encouraging research in this field by any method.

With the purpose of testing the effect of training on the validity of voice identification by aural and spectrographic examination of speech samples, as well as the effect of minority group voices, sex, and a half-year lapse between known and "unknown" samples, the following experiment was performed (Tosi and Greenwald, 1978). Twenty-five female and 25 male talkers, randomly selected from a Chicano population of Lansing, Michigan, recorded twice through commercial telephone lines four sentences (approximately 2.4 sec duration each) in Spanish. All recordings were produced from the home telephones of the subjects to the laboratory telephone. This telephone was attached to a magnetic toroid pick-up, connected to a cassette tape recorder. The first recording of each subject was done in quiet. The second recording consisted of two repetitions of the same sentences as in the first recording, one repetition done in quiet and the other with environmental noise at approximately 0 S/N ratio. The noise was produced by a radio or a television set at the residence of the subjects. The S/N ratio was measured at the laboratory end telephone by using a B&K artificial ear and a sound level meter. The two recording sessions were held approximately 6 months apart.

The cassette tapes containing these materials were dubbed onto open reel tapes at 7 1/2 ips, full track. With these master tapes spectrograms and aural materials for the experiment were prepared. The four subject recordings from the first call were used to prepare "known" speaker materials. Recordings from the second calls were utilized as "unknown" speaker materials. Therefore, three types of spectrograms and loop cartridge magnetic tapes were obtained from each subject: 1) "known" spectrograms and loop tapes; 2) "unknown" spectrograms and loop tapes in a noisy condition; and 3) "unknown" spectrograms and loop tapes in a quiet condition.

Spectrograms prepared with the voice samples were the bar, broadband type, within a range of 100 to 4,000 Hz, lineal scale,

---

[4] Also see letter of 23 March 1973 from the President of the Acoustical Society of America to the Executive Assistant U.S. Prosecutor (p. 144, Chapter 5).

obtained with a Voiceprint 700 spectrograph. Each subject yielded 12 spectrograms (one per sentence). The loop tapes consisted of 4-track endless cartridges, 60-sec duration. Each sentence was rerecorded on each of the 4-track cartridges; thus, each subject yielded three 4-track loop cartridges. Each track include one sentence, repeated through the whole duration of the loop.

With all these materials, three types of voice identification tests were prepared: 1) trials of voice identification by visual examination of a talker's spectrograms; 2) trials of voice identification by aural examination of a talker's voice; and 3) trials of voice identification by combined aural and spectrographic examination of a talker's samples. All trials of voice identification were of the discrimination match/no-match type. The researchers included 50% of "match" and 50% "no-match" tests for each examiner, randomly arranged.

The total number of tests made by each examiner were as follows: aural examination, 100 tests (50 in quiet conditions, 50 in noisy conditions); visual examination, 100 tests (50 in quiet conditions, 50 in noisy conditions); aural and visual examination, 100 tests (50 in quiet conditions, 50 in noisy conditions). The examiners were requested to express an opinion as to whether or not the unknown voice in each case was the same as or different than the known voice. Furthermore, they qualified their opinion with a percentage rating of self-confidence, from 51% to 100%. Examiners were also allowed to express no opinion one way or the other (by qualifying their answers with 50% probability).

Examiners consisted of two categories; 1) students of audiology and speech sciences who received approximately 1 week of training on spectrography prior to starting the experiment (these students were not selected according to a criterion for testing their ability to perform this type of task); and 2) professional examiners certified by the International Association of Voice Identification (IAVI).

Results from this study, presented in Tables 3a and b, suggest that: 1) training of examiners is crucial for validity of results of a subjective method of voice identification based on aural and spectrographic examination of talker samples; 2) sex, 6 months time elapsed between known and unknown talker samples, and minority group voices do not produce significant errors of voice identification provided that the examiner is a professionally trained person who uses no-opinion decisions and low percentage ratings of self-confidence when necessary, according to his/her professional judgment; 3) voice samples distorted by noise yielded a larger percentage of

Table 3a. Identification of minority group voices (results from untrained examiners, within a 90-100% self-confidence level)

Type of examination[a]	Quiet samples[b]		Noisy samples[c]	
	Range	Average	Range	Average
Errors of elimination (percentage)				
Visual:	0-5	1.70	0-9	2.90
No opinion:	0-11	2.40	0-9	2.50
Aural:	0-8	4.80	0-14	4.10
No opinion:	0-10	1.70	0-7	2.40
Aural-visual:	0-5	1.40	0-8	2.40
No opinion:	0-10	1.30	0-6	1.80
Errors of identification (percentage)				
Visual:	0-7	1.40	0-3	1.60
No opinion:	0-10	1.80	0-6	2.50
Aural:	0-9	1.50	0-13	2.40
No opinion:	0-5	1.20	0-8	2.30
Aural-visual:	0-1	0.40	0-6	1.50
No opinion:	0-3	0.80	0-4	1.30
Total average correct responses (minus both errors, percentage)				
Aural:		96.85		96.75
Visual:		98.45		97.75
Aural-visual:		99.10		98.05

[a] 100 trials per method.

[b] Average percent answers: elimination, 41.6%; identification, 50.6%.

[c] Average percent answers: elimination, 30.0%; identification, 41.0%.

errors of voice elimination and voice identification from untrained or laboratory examiners and a larger percentage of no-opinion decisions from professional examiners; and 4) untrained (laboratory) examiners produced a wide range of errors, according to their specific innate ability for this type of task. Indeed, for the same tests some laboratory examiners produced as low as 0-2% errors and other examiners up to 36% errors.

It is to be noted that the larger error average produced in this study, as compared with the error average produced in the Tosi et al. (1972) experiment in voice identification, could be explained by the fact that in the present study there was no selection of laboratory examiners according to a criterion, whereas in the former study laboratory examiners were selected according to a criterion of abil-

Table 3b. Identification of minority group voices (results from professional examiners, within a 90-100% self-confidence level)

Type of examination[a]	Quiet samples[b]		Noisy samples[c]	
	Range	Average	Range	Average
Errors of elimination (percentage)				
Visual:	0-0	0.00	0-0	0.00
No opinion:	29-34	31.50	39-45	42.00
Aural:	0-2	1.00	0-3	1.50
No opinion:	0-24	6.00	0-35	17.50
Aural-visual:	0-0	0.00	0-0	0.00
No opinion:	4-7	5.50	24-25	24.50
Errors of identification (percentage)				
Visual:	0-0	0.00	0-0	0.00
No opinion:	17-19	18.00	29-37	33.00
Aural:	0-3	1.50	0-3	1.60
No opinion:	0-22	11.00	0-32	16.00
Aural-visual:	0-0	0.00	0-0	0.00
No opinion:	1-9	5.00	10-24	17.00
Total average correct responses (minus both errors, percentage)				
Aural:		98.50		98.40
Visual:		100.00		100.00
No opinion:		100.00		100.00

[a] 100 trials per method.

[b] Average percent answers: elimination, 40.0%; identification, 45.0%.

[c] Average percent answers: elimination, 19.0%; identification, 23.0%.

ity to perform subjective identification tasks with 96% or more correct decisions in simpler tests.

More information on these matters can be found in the section on "Legality of Voice Identification From December 1970 to the Present" in Chapter 5.

In sum, subjective methods of voice identification might offer a reasonable degree of validity if properly applied to practical cases by trained examiners. Distortions produced by transmission and recording systems, background noise, and psychological and physiological conditions of talkers will greatly decrease the percentage of cases in which a positive identification could be reached. They will increase the percentage of no-opinion decisions or at the worst will increase the percentage of false eliminations. However, the same statements can be applied to objective methods of voice identification when they become sufficiently developed to be applicable to forensic cases. Other techniques of subjective identification widely used with no opposition, such as fingerprinting, handwriting analysis, etc., are also subject to similar restrictions. A latent fingerprint distorted by rubbing, paint, superimposed prints, etc., can only lead to a no-opinion decision.[5]

OBJECTIVE METHODS OF VOICE IDENTIFICATION

Objective methods of voice identification are those in which a decision as to whether or not an unknown and a known voice belong to the same talker is produced by a machine, specifically a computer, rather than directly by a human examiner.

This definition might not be accepted by some readers who would object that a computer still must be programmed and its output interpreted by a person. This is a valid objection; nevertheless, the author finds that such a definition is an acceptable operational one that satisfies a practical semantic need.

However, it is important to emphasize that the word "objective" should *not* be equated with "free of error." Indeed in many cases subjective methods could yield far less error than objective ones. The real assets of objective methods reside in their consistency and in the possibility of an accurate determination of the margin of errors, whether of identification or elimination.

Objective methods can be classified into two groups: *semiautomatic* and *automatic*. Semiautomatic methods need a large and continuous interaction of an examiner with the computer. In the automatic methods human interaction is limited; usually it consists of preparing and inputting proper samples as well as interpreting output from the computer.

Methods of *voice authentication* are a special case of automatic methods. Authentication methods consist of storing in the memory bank of a computer a set of features from the voices of a limited population of talkers (10 or so) who have recorded a short sample, usually a phoneme or a word. The computer compares features from a similar voice sample uttered by a challenging talker who

---

[5] This information was given to the writer by Detective Eugene Staelens, fingerprint expert from the Michigan Department of State Police, who added that in many cases latent fingerprints are simply not usable.

claims to be one of the talkers whose voice is stored. A decision algorithm follows; the computer will output a "same" or, alternatively, a "different" ruling. This system could be used to gain access to a restricted area, to confidential files, etc.

Voice authentication systems represent a simplification of automatic methods of voice identification in two aspects: 1) unknown and known voices are transmitted and recorded over the same channels; therefore, the influence of different response curves is eliminated; and 2) voice authentication is text-dependent, but enjoys the advantages of text-independent circumstances, because the challenging talker will use a prescribed utterance for purposes of authentication. In addition, the brief utterance required is produced with good articulation and clarity, quite different from most speech samples available as evidence in forensic cases of voice identification.

In objective methods of voice identification, a variety of approaches were and are being experimented with. The general steps of all different strategies are: a) selecting a suitable talker population as well as the type and duration of speech samples to be used; b) extracting efficient speech parameters from these samples; c) comparing similar parameters from the unknown and known samples by some type of algorithm, usually Euclidean distances; and d) adopting a decision criterion concerning the probability of an unknown and a known sample being from the same or from different talkers.

These operations are presently completed by digital computers. Proper computer programs can simulate all electronic analog instruments necessary for plotting speech spectra, extracting features, comparing similar features from unknown and known samples, etc. Digital input to the computer is usually obtained through a peripheral analog/digital translating device. Tape-recorded samples are played back in a tape recorder connected to the peripheral analog-digital (A/ D) device, which samples the speech wave temporally at a rate per second equal to double the frequency range desired. In other words, if the selected range of frequencies for analyzing the speech samples is 60 to 5,000 Hz, the A/D device must read intensities of the speech wave at about 10,000 times per second. These intensity readings are input in digital form to the computer to be processed according to the program prepared. Similar operations were performed with analog instruments in the near past at a tremendous cost of time and effort; now they are completed rather easily within a relatively short time by the computer.

Speech samples used for objective methods of voice identification could vary from long segments of different contexts of a large number of voice samples (text-independent methods) to a fixed phoneme uttered by a small number of collaborative talkers (voice authentication methods).

Efficient parameters for voice identification can be extracted from the time domain speech wave (linear prediction coefficient methods), from short-term spectra, or from the long-term spectrum (choral method).

Comparing similar parameters from unknown and known voices could be based on computing their Euclidean distances or submitting envelopes of spectra to a hierarchical algorithm or reducing sets of parameters to central tendency statistical or correlation measures, etc. Criteria for decision are usually developed by determining the boundaries of a space determined by selected parameters from the known speaker. An unknown voice sample should fall within that space to attain the desired probability that it belongs to the known talker. All these different approaches present advantages and disadvantages; the optimal objective method has not yet been found. Many of the studies have yielded a large percentage of correct identifications using samples spoken directly into a tape recorder; however, these studies have shown a much lesser degree of success with samples obtained through the telephone line.

At the present time no objective method is being used for examining voice evidence in a court of law; in the future they will certainly be used. A description of some research studies available in objective methods of voice identification follows. This section is not intended to be exhaustive or critical; the object is to bring to the nonspecialist reader a simplified review of studies in this area and their potentiality.

Semiautomatic Methods of Voice Identification

Most of these methods are text-dependent. That is, the examiner has to select from the unknown and known samples similar phonemes, syllables, or words to be compared. Although this selection is done by a person and not a computer, problems of alignment very often arise in semiautomatic methods; in other words it is no simple task to properly segment similar sounds to be compared from unknown and known samples.

After the computer processes these samples, extracts parameters, and analyzes them according to the particular program adopted, it produces an output. This output has to be interpreted by the examiner, who finally makes the decision as to whether the voices compared belong to same or different talkers.

One of the earliest studies on semiautomatic methods of voice identification was published by Pruzanski (1966). This was a text-dependent system using parameters extracted from the short-term spectra of talkers' samples. A total of 10 talkers (7 male and 3 female) recorded 4 utterances of 10 isolated words. These samples were processed through 17 band pass filters, within the frequency range of 100 to 7,000 Hz, yielding a word-utterance per speaker ratio as a function of time. Spectra from three utterances of the same word produced by each talker were combined to produce a talker definition pattern. The fourth utterance produced by every talker was then compared with each talker definition pattern. Product-moment correlations from these matchings were computed for 393 tests. A correct identification was considered to have been made if the maximum correlation obtained corresponded to actual matching utterances from the same talker. The range of correct identifications was from 74% to 97% depending on the particular word used to compute the statistical correlation. Recordings for this experiment were obtained directly (no telephone line involved). There were problems of temporal alignment with the words used. This experiment, using analog instruments rather than a computer, was very promising at that time in spite of the relatively low percentage of correct identifications obtained and its strong text-dependent characteristics.

In a semiautomatic method developed by Stanford Research Institute (Becker et al., 1972), sample speech waves were played back and displayed in a large TV monitor set. Through a suitable electronic device the examiner selected particular similar phonetic events from the voice samples to be compared. Six vowels from 100 talker samples were used in this experiment. The selected vowels were digitalized by an analog/digital translating device, and 64 linear prediction coefficients (Atal and Hanahuer, 1974) were extracted from each of these samples using a computer programmed with a suitable algorithm. Therefore, 384 (64 × 6) parameters characterized each experimental talker. Each talker was compared with himself and with the others by matching the 100 sets of 384 parameters. These matchings were performed by using four different alternative statistical techniques: uniform weighting, F-ratio, $1/\sigma$ weighting, and likelihood ratio. This last method proved to be better than the others. To produce decisions as to whether the two talkers compared were the same or different, the operator selected a threshold. Variation of the value of the threshold was correlated with different percentages of the probability of producing the correct identification. As an illustration, a threshold that yielded 100% correct identification in match tests also yielded 38% false identifications in no-match tests. In other words, for every 100 match discrimination trials, the 100 decisions were correct (talkers judged as being the same were the same), but for every 100 no-match discrimination trials judged under the same threshold, 38 decisions were false identifications (talkers judged as being the same actually being different). To have a 0% probability of false identifications with the best decision method (likelihood ratio), it is necessary to accept a 76% probability of false eliminations.

The authors concluded that the system could yield 1% errors of false identification providing that no decisions one way or the other are produced 30% of the time, and that recordings of "reasonably good quality" are available, containing the vowels /i/, /u/, /ɔ/, /ɪ/, /a/, /æ/ in the same syllabic content.

A companion to this study was the one subcontracted with Texas Instruments, Inc. and performed by Hair and Rekieta (1972). These authors employed a system similar to the one already discussed but using a population of up to 32 talkers and a maximum of 9 utterances of the same vowel from each talker.

Six vowels per talker were used as phonetic materials. From open voice identification tests performed with their talker population, the authors concluded that the system can attain a high degree of accuracy with only 1% of false identification probability, including a variable percentage of no-opinion decisions that depended on the open trial composition (number of talkers and whether or not it was a match or a no-match type). Another interesting conclusion was that the errors decrease with the increase of the number of utterances of the same phonetic element by the same talker. Also, it was concluded that some groups of talkers are more difficult to discriminate than other groups.

One significant study in semiautomatic methods was performed by the Aerospace Corporation (1977) of El Segundo, California. This study, called SASIS (Semi Automatic Speaker Identification System), was contracted in 1973 with the National Institute of Law Enforcement and Criminal Justice (U.S. Department of Justice). The program was terminated in 1976 by the Institute before some recommended improvements in the system would have taken place. Hardware for this project, essentially a minicomputer and a peripheral A/D device as well as some software, were subcontracted with Rockwell International.

The SASIS consisted of matching steady phonetic segments from the same text uttered by one unknown and several known persons. Optimal parameters or features selected for these matchings were: fundamental frequencies, density of zero crossings, and linear prediction coefficients (from the time domain speech wave); and mean frequencies, bandwidths of formants, power spectrum density amplitudes, and slopes (from the frequency domain speech wave). Ten pairs of phonetic events from the samples were compared in the experimental trials. The researchers found that comparisons of vowels and nasal consonants yielded the smallest number of errors.

In this system the examiner has to select the pair of similar sounds from the unknown and known talkers to be analyzed by the computer in each case. Therefore, the examiner has to be a person trained in phonetics in order to be able to produce such a selection. Once the similar phonetic events are selected by listening to the samples and performing a phonetic transcription, samples are fed into the analog/digital translating device of the minicomputer for processing. The computer is programmed to extract 30 features from each phonetic event to be compared. Then the Euclidean distances of these 30 pairs of features are computed. Sets of distances are combined to obtain a final number that indicates the difference between the talker samples compared. The examiner then has to consult a statistical table that will specifically disclose the probability that the samples compared belong to the same talker.

The experimental trials in this study were performed using speakers of three different English dialects: General American English, Black Urban, and Chicano. Both male and female talkers were utilized. Errors of false identification were 3% on the average when telephone lines were not used to obtain the recordings. Telephone line recordings proved to interact strongly with the system, however, rendering the method not useful for the courtroom application intended by the contracting agency. Several options were considered to overcome the effect of the telephone response curve, but because the U.S. Department of Justice terminated the contract, funds were not available to pursue the study.

In concluding this discussion on semiautomatic methods, the

author would like to report an experiment in progress that he is presently conducting with his associates, Drs. Richard Dubes and Jaim Anil. This method consists of scanning spectrograms of the same context from the unknown and known voices through a digitalizing optical device. This instrument is capable of quantifying point by point the speech power density through the whole area of each spectrogram. Sets of numbers obtained in this manner, representing each talker, are fed into a minicomputer. Suitable algorithms for feature extraction and decision production are programmed. A number of discrimination trials, using the same population of talkers utilized for the experiment reported in Tosi et al., 1972 (see "Aural Examination of Voices" section), are scheduled to be tested. Probabilities of error will be obtained from these experimental trials. To further test the system, samples from practical cases will be submitted to the same type of processing. A final evaluation of all results will indicate whether or not this system has practical applications.

Automatic Methods of Voice Identification

A brief description of five studies in automatic methods of voice identification, in chronological order, follows. In these systems there is a variable degree of human interaction with the computer; but because the respective researchers have labeled them as "automatic methods," this author has decided to keep that labeling even if in some instances the word "semiautomatic" would be more proper to designate some of these studies.

Atal (1972) published a study in which the parameters used to identify a talker consisted of the temporal variations of pitch, or rather of the glottal frequency—the characteristic melody curve of the talker. Atal indicated that this type of parameter for speaker identification presents two main advantages over other parameters, such as those derived from spectral patterns. One advantage is that the melody curve is not affected by the response curve of the transmitting and recording system. The second advantage is that an imposter might have difficulty trying to mimic the melody curve of a given talker. Atal used 10 female talkers for this study who had a close average habitual glottal frequency. They recorded twice, with a 27-day interval, a set of five different sentences that were repeated in a random fashion six times in total. Only one of these sentences (including only voiced phonemes) was actually used for the study. The other four sentences were used just to prevent the talkers from introducing any special emphasis into the clue sentence when recording it—they did not know which was the clue sentence.

Phonetic materials utilized in this study consisted of 60 samples of the same sentence (6 repetitions by 10 talkers) with a duration of 1.8 to 2.8 sec, according to each particular speaker. Five utterances per talker were used to extract parameters for producing a reference vector to characterize each talker. The sixth utterance of each talker was used as the "unknown" sample to be compared with 10 "known" reference vectors. In other words, the tests performed by Atal were the closed type.

Recordings for this experiment were obtained directly (no telephone line involved) through high quality equipment. Samples were digitalized by means of a peripheral A/D device and subsequently the melody curves for each speaker were extracted by using a special algorithm programmed in a digital computer. By averaging the melody curves or "pitch contours" from 5 utterances of each talker, and finally reducing these data to 20-dimension vectors, each talker was so characterized. A similar 20-dimension vector per talker was produced with the sixth utterance. Next, each one of these "unknown" talker vectors was compared with the 10 "known" vectors by computing their respective Euclidean distances. The "unknown" speaker with the smallest Euclidean distance to any of the "known" talkers was selected as being the same. The percentage of correct identifications found in this manner was 97%. Atal concluded that "pitch contours" are efficient parameters for automatic talker identification. In some ways, but not completely, this conclusion contradicts the one by Coleman (1973), reported in the section on "Aural Examination of Voices."

Wolf (1972) approached the problem of automatic speaker identification by testing different sets of significant parameters, searching for the most efficient set, that is, the one that could provide a minimum intratalker variability and a maximum intertalker variability. In addition he attempted to select these parameters from among the usual ones in acoustic and phonological theories of speech. This was a text-dependent experiment in which the particular phonetic events selected for parameter extraction had to be located on a CRT display by visual examination of the operator. After this localization was completed, the measurement of the selected parameters was performed by a digital computer (a PDP-9) according to a suitable program. Samples were obtained from 21 male adult talkers with an age range of 22 to 42 years, all speaking

the General American English dialect with no distinctive peculiar-
ities except for minor regional accents. Samples consisted of 10
repetitions of 6 short sentences recorded directly (no telephone line
involved) through high quality equipment. All samples were contemporary. Wolf tested combinations of up to about 27 parameters
extracted from nasal consonants, vowel spectra, glottal frequency
and glottal sources spectrum slope, word duration, and voice onset
gaps. Discrimination decisions were based on computation of Euclidean distances among similar parameters of "unknown" and
"known" samples. A 2% error of false identification in closed tests
was produced using optimal combination of the parameters selected
as the most efficient ones.

Su and Fu (1973) published a text-dependent study on automatic talker identification based on decision criteria derived from
parameters extracted alternatively from spectra of nasal consonants, of words excerpted from a sentence, and of continuous
speech. Spectra of nasal consonants proved to be the most useful
of the three alternatives and spectra from excerpted words the least
useful. These researchers used readings from 10 talkers (5 male and
5 female) as phonetic materials to test their system, processed by
means of a digital computer. In closed tests of voice identification
correct responses ranging from 100% to 10% were found, according
to the phonetic materials and decision algorithm used. In their
report the authors included a complete review of the available
literature on automatic speaker identification up to 1973.

Also, Atal (1974) conducted another experiment using linear
prediction coefficients and ceptrum as effective parameters for an
automatic speaker identification. The linear predictor coefficients
were discussed in a paper by Atal and Schroeder (1970).

Briefly, segments from a talker's speech, combined in suitable
linear equations, allow the prediction of the waveshape of subsequent segments of that talker's speech. Ceptrum is an algorithm
defined as the inverse Fourier transform of the logarithm of the
transfer function of the talker's vocal tract (see the section on
"Fourier Transforms" in Chapter 2). Atal used for this experiment
10 talkers who recorded twice, with about a 1-month interval, three
utterances of a short sentence. Recordings were made directly into
a tape recorder using high quality equipment, but the range of
frequencies extended only up to 5,000 Hz. For extraction of 12
linear prediction coefficients and ceptrum computation, sample sentences were divided into 40 segments. Five utterances from each

talker were used to derive a reference vector; the sixth utterance was utilized to derive similar parameters to be compared against the reference vectors of all 10 talkers. A decision criterion as to whether or not two talkers compared were the same or different was based on a non-Euclidean distance between their two vectors, computed according to the equations suggested by Shafer and Rabiner (1975). This experiment by Atal, strongly text-dependent, yielded, for the best alternative vector derivation with the parameters he used, a 95% probability of correct identifications. Ceptrum vector proved to have the best discrimination potential; possibly it was due to the fact that the influence of the response curve of the transmitting and recording medium could be easily eliminated from the ceptrum function, provided that it is reliably known that samples are of short duration. This possible use of ceptrum would be outstanding for practical cases, where evidence is usually obtained through telephone communications; the problem is that the response curve of the telephone line used to record the evidence in most cases cannot be determined.

Li and Hughes (1974) published a study dealing with talker differences as they appear in correlation matrices of the long-term spectra of continuous speech. They measured the differences between any combination of two matrices from a population of 30 talkers. Intratalker difference was defined as the difference between matrices obtained from spectra of similar texts read by the same talker and intertalker difference was defined as the difference between matrices obtained from spectra of the same text read by different talkers. The results indicated that there is only a 1% overlap in the distribution of these differences that might confuse absolute identification of a given talker. Recordings of phonetic materials for this study were obtained directly using high quality equipment. The spectra were processed by a digital computer which then extracted the matrices.

Hollien and Majewski (1977) produced a study on text-independent automatic talker identification using long-term spectra from samples to extract features for talker discrimination. There were two experiments performed. The first used "normal" voices of 25 male Americans and 25 male Poles reading a 2.5-min duration passage in English and in Polish respectively. Recordings were examined directly using good quality equipment. Long-term spectra were obtained from these 50 samples using a digital computer simulating 23 one-third octave band filters covering a range from 80 to 12,500 Hz.

Three 32-sec segments from each talker were combined to form a reference pattern; the fourth segment was used as an "unknown" sample for tests of voice identification. Euclidean distances computed from 23-dimensional space parameters extracted from the long-term spectra from each talker were utilized as a talker identification criterion.

In 96% of the tests for the Americans and in 94% of the tests for the Poles, Euclidean distances were the smallest between samples from the same talker, thus yielding a correct identification.

The second experiment utilized essentially the same method as the first one but the talkers were only Americans. They read the text in three conditions: a) normal voice; b) under "stress;" and c) disguised voice. The long-term spectra of the normal voice samples were used as a reference ("known" samples). The spectra from the stressed or disguised voice samples were used as "unknown" samples. In this experiment the percentage of correct identification in all discrimination tests performed decreased to 92%.

In both experiments voice samples were filtered to a narrow band of frequencies: 315 to 3,150 Hz (close to telephone line response) was tested. With this restricted band of frequencies, percentages of correct identification decreased to 82% (Americans) and 70% (Poles) in the first experiment. The second experiment yielded 72% correct identification under this restricted condition.

Tosi and his associates have recently taken a somewhat new approach to automatic methods of voice identification. Briefly, the system used is text-independent (even language-independent) and consists of the hierarchical grouping of talkers' choral spectra. Choral spectra are the long-term Fourier transforms of temporal choral speech, as defined by Tarnoczy (1958). Choral speech from a talker consists of a temporal rearrangement of his normal speech. A concrete example might serve as illustration of this definition. Assume a talker recorded a 300-sec long speech on a magnetic tape. This tape is then segmented into 60 portions of 5-sec duration each. Each of these portions is placed on a tape recorder; these 60 tape recorders are connected to a mixer and the mixer to another tape recorder containing a blank tape. Then all tape recorders are turned on simultaneously. Tape recorders 1 through 60 will each play their 5-sec tape into the mixer; tape recorder 61 will record on the blank tape the common output from the mixer. Therefore, this mixed recording will consist of a 5-sec choral speech from the talker voice. Such a choral speech would convey to a listener a perception similar to listening to 60 talkers simultaneously speaking different texts; the difference is that in choral speech the voice belongs to only one person (Figure 3.4).

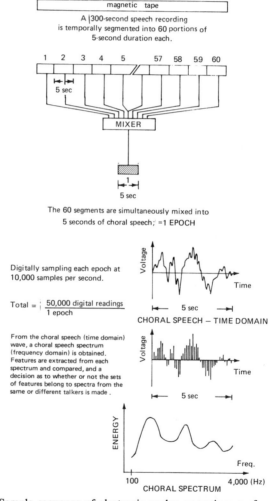

Figure 3.4. Sample sequence of electronic analog operations performed to obtain choral spectra from a speech sample.

Of course, there is no need to use all these tape recorders to obtain choral speech. They were mentioned only for the sake of clarification. There are available special loop-tape devices, such as the Sanborn 3917 FM tape recorder, that are better suited to the task. It is even more convenient, easier, and faster to obtain choral speech spectra by using a digital minicomputer rather than analog instruments. The author and his associates have used both alternatives.

The preceding explanation might have brought to the attention of the reader the strong text-independent characteristic of the choral method. Even different languages spoken by the same talker could be processed and compared by adopting the proposed method. This feature is most useful for forensic applications of voice identification; indeed obtaining voice samples from suspected persons is often very difficult or impractical if the same text employed by the unknown talker must be used, but it could be rather simple to obtain samples of suspects' voices if the text were not a restricting consideration.

Returning to the general description of the choral method: once the previous task is completed, the next step consists of obtaining the long-term Fourier spectrum from the choral speech wave of each talker involved. From each choral long-term spectrum a number of features are extracted to represent each talker in a multidimensional space. These features are subsequently processed according to a special hierarchical algorithm from which several clusters result. A correct identification is obtained if the choral spectrum of the unknown talker is clustered with the choral spectra of other samples from the same talker; a false identification is produced if it is clustered with different talkers' choral spectra in a match, open trial experiment. Alternatively, in no-match experiments (i.e., when an unknown talker is actually none of the "known" ones) a correct result is obtained if the choral spectrum of the unknown talker is placed outside of the clusters formed by those of the known talkers.

As of this writing two pilot experiments have been performed by the author using this choral method. In the first one[6] (Bordone et al., 1974), analog instruments were utilized to obtain choral

---

[6] This experiment was initiated in 1973 during the author's sabbatical leave, spent at the Department of Acoustics of the Institute Galileo Ferraris of Torino, Italy. The author is very grateful to the Director, Dr. Sacerdote, and staff for the excellent suggestions and support received.

speech and spectra from 20 talkers (14 male, 6 female) who produced a total of 180 10-min samples. These talkers produced their samples using three different languages (Piamontes, Italian, and French) in three recording sessions spaced a week apart. Nine 20-sec choral speech samples were obtained from each talker by using a Sanborn tape recorder. Correlated choral spectra were processed with a B&K 2107 analyzer and its associate instruments (Figure 3.5). Choral spectra were plotted with a B&K Level Recorder 2305. The range of frequencies used was 63 to 6,300 Hz, including one intensity ordinate every 0.04 octave; that is, a total of 156 ordinates per spectrum (see Figure 2.11). Intensities were plotted in dB relative to an arbitrary zero, at -25 dB from a common peak value.

These spectra were transferred to computer cards and processed through a hierarchical clustering algorithm, implemented on the CDC 6500 computer at Michigan State University. Various alternative computations for clustering spectra matrices (each containing 156 features per talker) were explored. Errors of false identification ranged from 30% to 5%, according to the alternative computation selected.

The main conclusion to be drawn from this pilot experiment is that each speaker possesses relative invariances in his/her choral spectrum, irrespective of the text or language spoken. Possibly the same statement could be applied to long-term spectra from normal

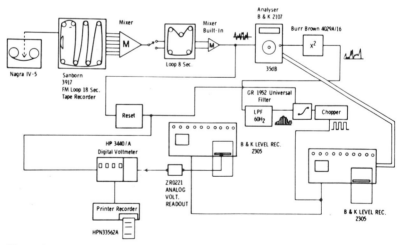

Figure 3.5. Analog system actually used to obtain choral spectra in Bordone et al. experiment (1974).

speech; however, it is necessary to have a very long speech sample to have any success with that type of spectra. Use of choral spectra saves effort and cuts computer time by a factor of 20 or so, yielding in addition better results than the normal speech long-term spectra because it seems that the response curve of the recording channels does not affect the former as much as it affects the latter. It should be noted that the extra time necessary to obtain choral speech from normal speech become negligible with respect to the total time necessary to complete the voice identification examination.

A second pilot experiment (Tosi et al., 1977) was carried out with the main goal of computerizing the whole operation previously described. The same raw data from the first experiment were used. Original samples were played into a tape recorder connected to an peripheral analog/digital device attached to a PDP 11/40 minicomputer. Speech waves were digitally sampled by the peripheral A/D device at the rate of 10,000 intensity readings per second, thus allowing the speech range of frequencies to be kept approximately between 60 Hz and 5,000 Hz. A suitable program yielded choral speech and sequential choral spectra from each sample input, almost in real time. These spectra included one intensity ordinate over each 0.06 octave band width, that is, a total of 76 ordinates per spectrum. Intensities were plotted in dB relative to an arbitrary zero at −60 dB from a common peak. Choral spectra were plotted in hard copies (Figure 3.6) and also transferred by an interfacing device to the CDC 6500 computer.

Here a process similar to the one utilized in the first experiment, but including some improvements, took place. Results yielded no errors of grouping or false identifications. To illustrate these results, two different graphs were prepared, a Shepperd graph (by reducing the 76 parameters per speaker to a 2-dimensional space) and a minimum spanning tree vectoral diagram. Samples of these graphs are shown in Figures 3.7a and 3.7b.

Further experimentation with this choral method is presently in progress at the Michigan State University Institute of Voice Identification. Goals are now to investigate the effects of different types of telephone lines and recording channels, noise, low quality recordings, mimicking and disguising, and time elapsed between unknown and known voice recordings. Practical cases examined previously with subjective spectrographic methods are also scheduled for processing with this automatic choral method.

In conclusion, automatic methods of voice identification are

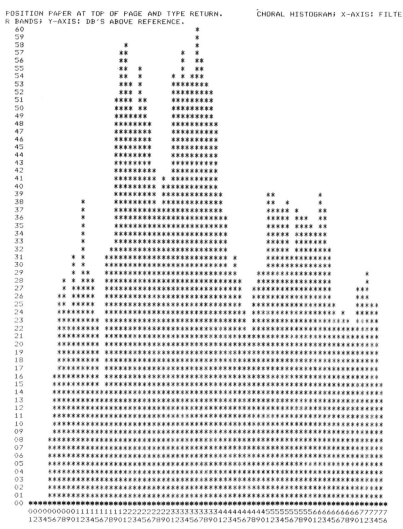

Figure 3.6. Choral speech spectrum from one talker, uttering a 20-sec speech in French, obtained from the computer (hard copy).

still not well enough developed to be applicable to forensic cases. One of the problems to overcome is the influence of the transmitting and recording channels, noise, and other distortions of the voice samples. Automatic methods provide high percentages of correct identifications only with very aseptic samples and a small population

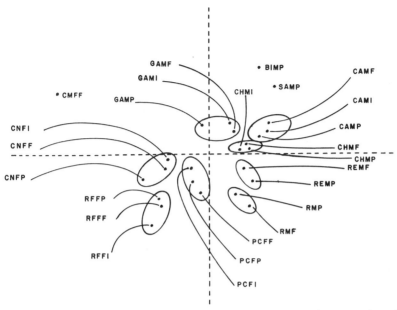

Figure 3.7a. Shepperd diagram from hierarchical grouping of 11 talkers, 6 male and 5 female, speaking up to three different languages. Subjects GA (male), CH (male), CA (male), CN (female), RF (female), and PC (female) spoke French, Italian, and Piamontes, in each recording. Subjects BI (male), and SA (male) spoke only Piamontes in each recording, and subject CM (female) spoke only French. Subjects RE (male) and RM (male) spoke French and Piamontes in each recording.

of voices. There is no doubt that further studies will greatly improve these methods and that they will find their way into courts of law. Possibly, a combination of subjective and objective methods used concurrently might expedite these practical applications. Whatever the case may be, the reader should realize that a trained practitioner will be necessary to obtain, analyze, and present the evidence in a court of law. Also, no method or combination of methods could ever solve 100% of the cases analyzed "beyond a reasonable doubt." For further elaboration of this subject see the section on "Future of Voice Identification" (Chapter 5).

PROBABILITY OF ERROR AND RECEIVER OPERATING CHARACTERISTIC IN VOICE IDENTIFICATION METHODS

No system of identification is exempt from presenting a probability of error. A given method might yield a negligible probability figure;

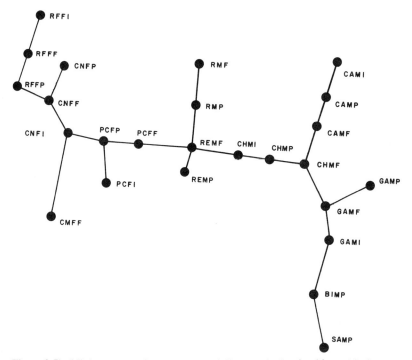

Figure 3.7b. Minimum spanning tree vectoral diagram, indicating hierarchical grouping of same subjects as in Figure 3.7a.

hence it is possible to assess such a method as a very safe one, but the statement "one hundred percent correct" is just a figure of speech; it is a mathematical impossibility whatever the method might be.

In this section a brief outline on decision theory is offered, together with an explanation of the receiver operating characteristic (ROC), a curve that can be plotted to disclose the quality of examinations performed by using any kind of method—by automatic devices or by human examiners.

To facilitate this explanation, only discrimination tasks for voice identification will be considered; in addition, it will be assumed that the system or examiner is not allowed to give a no-opinion decision.

Notions from the decision theory for discrimination trials can be extended easily to open trials. Concerning the effect of the no-opinion criterion, it is obvious that this effect will tend to decrease the errors obtained in case of forced "same"/"different" decisions. A quantitative estimation of the amount of that effect could present some theoretical problems; however, it can be stated that the percentage of errors would decrease at least proportionally to the percentage of no-opinion decisions. Clearly, if total percentage of errors under forced positive decisions is, for instance, 8%, with a no-opinion decision option this percentage could diminish proportionally to 4.8% if there were 40 no-opinion decisions for every 100 cases examined.

Probability of Error in Discrimination Tests

Concerning only discrimination trials with forced "same"/"different" decisions, let's assume 100 trials, including S number of cases in which the unknown talker is the same as the known talker, and D number of cases in which the unknown talker is different from the known talker. Further, let's assume that the examiner or computer has decided in s number of cases that the two voices compared were the same, and in d number of cases that they were different. Because *probability* is defined as the quotient of the actual number of events or decisions of some kind divided by the total possible number of events or decisions, it is immediately deduced that:

Probability of false identification   = $P(s/D)$

Probability of false elimination   = $P(d/S)$

Probability of correct identification = $P(s/S)$

Probability of correct elimination   = $P(d/D)$

and that:

$$P(s/D) + P(d/D) = 1 \qquad\qquad \text{(A)}$$

$$P(d/S) + P(s/S) = 1 \qquad\qquad \text{(B)}$$

Equation A indicates that the probability of false identification plus the probability of correct elimination is equal to one, that is, certainty. Equation B indicates that the probability of false elimination plus the probability of correct identification is equal to one, that is, certainty.

A numerical example will illustrate these properties. Assume 10 discrimination trials in which $S = 4$ matches and $D = 6$ no-matches. Further assume $s = 3$ "same" decisions and $d = 1$ "different" decision for the match trials, and $d = 4$ "different" decisions and $s = 2$ "same" decisions for the no-match trials. Applying the above equations:

$1/4 + 3/4 = 1$, or 25% probability of false identification + 75% probability of correct elimination = 100% of match trials

$2/6 + 4/6 = 1$, or 33⅓% probability of false elimination + 66⅔% probability of correct identification = 100% of no-match trials

As a consequence, it can be stated that, keeping all other circumstances equal, the only way to decrease the probability of false identification is to increase the probability of correct elimination, and the only way to decrease the probability of false elimination is to increase the probability of correct identification. It should be emphasized that these statements are mathematically correct only if "all other circumstances are kept equal," that is, the same quality of samples, the same method of voice identification, the same discriminating ability of the system or the examiner, etc.

Now, a compromising strategy must be adopted according to the cost of the different type of probabilities. For instance, if the legal and moral cost of false identifications cannot be afforded or tolerated, then a system that is not too sensitive to probability of producing false eliminations or alternatively correct identifications might be accepted, because these two probabilities are independent: one is constrained by Equation A, the other by Equation B. If our philosophy of justice demands that the probability of indicting an innocent person be kept as low as possible, then a low probability of producing correct eliminations might be accepted. For instance, a system might yield 14 correct identifications, one false identification, and five correct eliminations for every 100 tests. The remaining results (80) have to be false eliminations, according to Equations A and B. A researcher might report these results alternatively as: 1) correct results obtained with this method of voice identification were only 19%; or 2) errors of false identification obtained with this method were 1% and errors of false elimination 80%; correct identifications were 14% and correct eliminations were 5%. Alternative 1 will convey to the reader the notion that the system tested is not valid at all for legal uses; alternative 2 will rather support its legal usage if 1% of false identification is an acceptable risk and 80% of false elimination is deemed not too important or costly within a given philosophy of justice, or if these errors could be transformed into no-opinion decisions by better trained examiners than the ones used in that hypothetical laboratory experiment. A researcher must always follow alternative 2; otherwise it is difficult to properly interpret results as happens, in the opinion of this author, with the papers by Hollien and McGlone (1976) and Reich, Moll, and Curtis (1976).

Of course the probabilities are relative and the absolute values of errors could be very low, depending upon the factors previously enumerated; a good system of voice identification can produce a negligible probability of false identifications and a very large probability of correct identifications; but the sum of probabilities within Equation A and Equation B respectively is equal to 1, *always*, and both equations are independent.

Equations A and B also, in some way, quantify the aims of a prosecutor and a defense lawyer concerning the quality of voice identification evidence. Indeed, the prosecutor might request that the method used guarantee maximum probability of correct identifications; he is ruled, therefore, by Equation B, which presents no conflicts because false eliminations will be concurrently minimized. The defense counselor, on the other hand, wants the method that maximizes the probability of correct eliminations; he is ruled, therefore, by Equation A, which shows that maximizing correct elimination probabilities implies minimizing false identifications. Eventually both aims could conflict within a given system of voice identification because there is no functional relationship or constraint between Equations A and B. Clearly, a system that ensures excellent probabilities of correct identifications does not necessarily ensure excellent probabilities of correct eliminations.

These concepts, derived from discrimination decisions, can be extended to open trial decisions. Here, as explained in the section on "Types of Tests and Errors in Voice Identification and Elimination" (Chapter 1), errors of false identification have two possible sources: 1) a match did not exist, but an examiner selected one of the known talkers as the same as the unknown talker; and 2) a match did exist but an examiner selected the wrong known talker as being the same as the unknown one. This situation in voice identification is similar to the "line-up" situation in visual identification of suspects. This model should consequently be modified for application to discrimination equations. In a restricted way this was done by Starr et al. (1975); these authors have determined the relationship between the probabilities of correct identification in discrimination tasks and the probabilities of deciding that a match does exist in an open trial situation, if that is true (regardless of whether the wrong or right match is selected afterwards). Even if in the second stage of the open trials the wrong match is selected, this would not interfere with the relationship of probabilities already indicated. In this restricted way the property studied by Starr and associates is useful for plotting the ROC curve for open tests. Indeed, because there exists a known proportion between the probability of producing correct identifications in simple discrimination trials and the probability of deciding there is a match in open trials, an ROC curve for open trials could be plotted using the same technique as in simple discrimination trials. This curve discloses the quality of the examination. Dr. David M. Green, a professor at the Laboratory of Psychophysics at Harvard University, applied this method to data from the Tosi et al. (1972) experiment in voice identification with reliable results.

Receiver Operating Characteristic

The receiver operating characteristic (ROC) is a graph plotted with data obtained through special tests of voice identification to determine the discriminatory ability of a system or an examiner when known and unknown samples are compared and to decide whether they were produced by the same or by different talkers. This ROC graph might be used to obtain information on the probability of a voice identification examiner's conclusions being correct in an actual case, whatever method is used to make the conclusions. Also, ROC can be utilized for the same purpose to test a computer algorithm applied to automatic talker identification, etc. The testing samples necessary to plot the ROC must be: a) experimental, i.e., the identity of the "unknown" sample has to be known to the person plotting the ROC for testing a given examiner or system, and b) equivalent in quality and conditions, comparable to samples from practical situations, if conclusions from the ROC plottings are intended for application to real-life cases.

The operator of the system should adopt a scale of different degrees of self-confidence in judging or different criteria of likelihood for each decision. These different criteria for decisions must be specified by a scale consisting of a discrete number of points, such as:

4. Almost certain (or very high confidence) that samples are from the same subject
3. Fairly certain (or high confidence) that samples are from the same subject
2. Fairly certain that samples are from different subjects (or low confidence sample are from same subject)
1. Almost certain that samples are from different subject (or very low confidence sample are from same subject)

With results of all testing cases, the ROC curve for the particular examiner or system under study can be plotted as follows. For each point of the criterion scale utilized compute the number of cases of the examiner or system having decided ''same'' when this was true. Divide this number by the total number of cases presented to him/her actually containing a ''match.'' This ratio is the probability that this examiner or system (if all other conditions are kept constant) will produce correct identifications. Plot these probabilities along the vertical axis of the ROC graph. Probabilities calculated for each point of the criterion scale should be added sequentially along this axis.

For each point of the criterion scale utilized compute the number of cases the examiner (or system) has decided ''same'' when this was not true. Divide this number by the total number of cases presented to him/her actually containing a ''no-match.'' This ratio is the probability that this examiner or system (if all other conditions are kept constant) will produce false identifications. Plot these probabilities in an accumulative fashion along the horizontal axis of the ROC graph.

Each pair of probabilities (vertical and horizontal) determine a point of the ROC curve, which then can be plotted (Figure 3.8). The theoretical initial point of this curve is the origin of the axes (A) and the final point is (B), the intersection of 1.0 and 1.0 probabilities. It can be proved (Swetts, 1973) that the area enclosed by the curve ABC in Figure 3.8 is proportional to the relative quality or validity of the examiner's or system's decisions. The relative size of this area of course includes the quality of the samples themselves in addition to the intrinsic ability of the examiner or system to produce correct ''same'' or ''different'' decisions using these samples. If the same sets of samples are presented to different examiners, the area subtended by the ROC curve for each examiner shows proportion-

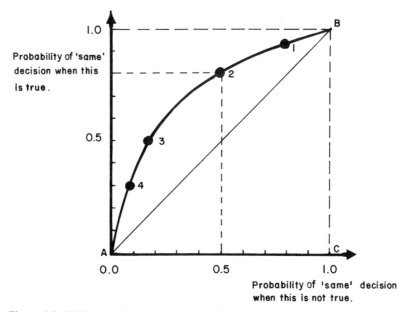

Figure 3.8. ROC curve from an examiner. The points on vertical axis represent accumulated percentages of "same" decisions when this was true, and the points on the horizontal axis represent accumulated percentages of "same" decisions when this was not true, in a series of discrimination tests. Points 1, 2, 3, and 4 indicate different decision criteria, from low to high self-confidence in the correctness of the decision.

ally his relative decision-making ability. In Figure 3.9 the upper curve belongs to examiner Y, possessing a better ability than examiner Z, who has yielded the lower curve from tests using the same samples as examiner Y used.

Two different examiners may have a different subjective interpretation of each point of the criterion scale and still yield the same ROC curve (Figure 3.10). The criteria for examiner S are represented by solid squares; the criteria for examiner R are represented by open squares. In spite of the difference in criteria, both examiners have the same amount of skill, as shown by the same area enclosed by the shared ROC curve.

It is interesting to note that the extreme points A and B of a ROC curve represent two extreme decision criteria. A represents the criterion for deciding that two samples are *never* from the same person. B represents the criterion for deciding that two samples are *always* from the same person. Therefore, using criterion A, the

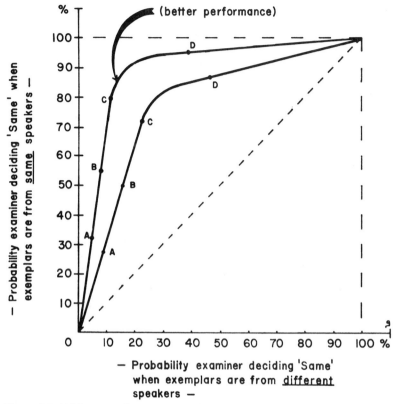

Figure 3.9. ROC curves from two examiners tested on the same materials. One examiner was more capable than the other examiner for those common tests.

probability the examiner will decide that the samples are the "same" (whether this is true or not) is zero, because with that criterion he will never say "same." The probability the examiner will decide "same" when using criterion B is one (maximum or certainty), irrespective of whether this is true or not, because with that criterion he will always say "same."

Another important conclusion that can be deduced from inspection of the ROC curve is that the only way to increase the probability of producing correct identifications is to be willing to increase the probability of false eliminations simultaneously. Of course that statement is mathematically true if the whole ROC for a given examiner cannot be improved by increasing the area comprised by the curve by some means, i.e., by adopting a different

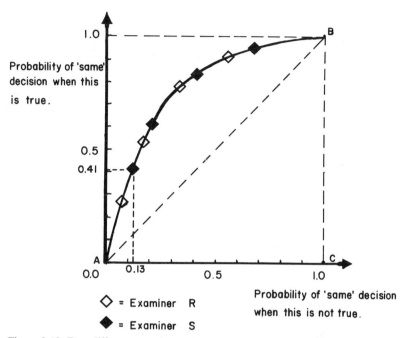

Figure 3.10. Two different examiners (R and S) produced the same quality of voice identification tests; however, their decision criteria, symbolized by white and black squares respectively, was different.

method of identification or simply by refusing to work with noisy, distorted samples or by adopting an alternative conclusion of "no decision one way or the other" after the examination is complete. This alternative conclusion is equivalent to screening the available samples and accepting only the better ones for testing to decide whether they originated from the same voice or not.

In sum, the ROC curve is a mathematical derivation of the theory of decisions that can greatly help to evaluate any aspect of the links that form the chain of events related to voice identification: the quality and validity of samples utilized, the method, the skill of the examiner, or the usefulness of the algorithm employed in automatic systems. Naturally the evaluation of any of these variables demands that all others are kept constant for the whole test performed to plot the ROC curve.

chapter 4

FIELD PRACTICE IN VOICE IDENTIFICATION BY AURAL AND SPECTROGRAPHIC EXAMINATION OF SPEECH SAMPLES

OVERVIEW OF FIELD PRACTICE IN VOICE IDENTIFICATION

Because voice identification by aural and spectrographic examination of speech samples is the only system presently used for obtaining voice identification evidence in legal cases, or simply for investigation of criminal cases involving the voice of the criminal, a description of the procedures followed by a practitioner of this field (as recommended by the International Association of Voice Identification (IAVI)) is presented in this chapter. Even if in the future subjective methods are partially or completely discarded, many of the operations here described still will be valid for any objective methods that could be used.

In the actual practice of voice identification and elimination there are several steps to be completed between the moment a criminal is using his/her voice in the commission of a crime and the moment that a suspected person is tried in a court of law, using his/her voice as the only or concurrent evidence for his/her conviction or acquittal.

The first step of the practice consists of recording the criminal call. The next step is to find individuals suspected of being the "unknown" caller and obtaining samples of their voices, using the same text as that in the criminal call. There exists a possibility that some future methods will not require use of the same text for matching samples. Such text-independent systems of voice identification can simplify (or in some cases even make possible) this step.

The next step consists of sending all the voice samples to a professional examiner of voice identification with as little information as possible on specifics of the case. It is also desirable to include voices other than those of suspected persons or defendants among the known voices to be compared with the criminal voice(s). In this case the known voices will be labeled with a number rather than with a name. The professional examiner will prepare suitable exemplars for voice examination from the samples received in order to perform the examination and to reach a decision for each pair of voices compared. The decision is based on decision criteria as adopted by the IAVI and explained in Chapter 3. Then, the agency or person responsible for the case should determine what to do with the examiner's decision. In some cases the evidence will be used in a trial, but in other cases it will not—for example, cases in which the prosecution has ordered the examination and the examiner decided that there was only a low probability that the criminal's voice was the same as the defendant's voice. A detailed discussion of each of the steps outlined follows.

RECORDING OF THE CRIMINAL CALL

There are several specific ways to obtain a recording of the call related to the commission of the crime. One is when an unknown person calls a police headquarters, a factory, a business office, etc., with a bomb threat, a false fire alarm, information connected with a crime, etc. Many police headquarters possess 24-hr tape recorders that record all incoming calls. The portion of the 24-hr tape that contains the criminal call is then transferred onto a cassette or an open reel magnetic tape. Usually the quality of the 24-hr tape is poor, but if the machine is properly maintained this recording is usable for purposes of identification or elimination. Transfer of the criminal call should be properly done, using a tape recorder connected through patching wires to the playback machine.

Some actual cases in which this manner of recording the unknown caller was used were:

Call to a police headquarters
  Minnesota v. *Constance Trimble*, Ramsey Co. District Ct., St.
    Paul, MN., No. 24,049 (1970)
  Michigan v. *Frederick Lemon*, 61st District Ct., Grand Rapids,
    MI. (1972)
  Michigan v. *Chaisson*, District 54-1, City of Lansing, MI.
    (1973)
Call to a factory
  U.S. v. *Betty Phoenix*, So. District Indiana, No. 70-Cr-428
    (1971)

A second way to obtain recordings of criminal calls is when
the unknown caller calls an individual or a private home with the
purpose of extortion, to request ransom money, or to make an
obscene call. In this case the victim may request the assistance of
the police. Usually, police properly instructed by a crime laboratory
will connect a tape recorder to the victim's telephone. The tape
recorder can be connected directly to the telephone line or through
a pick-up, i.e., a magnetic toroidal pick-up attached to the telephone
receiver. The tape recorder must be plugged into an electrical outlet
to avoid power failures due to use of low-voltage batteries. A clean
tape or cassette should always be available in the tape recorder and
the system should be tested frequently to prevent electrical or
mechanical problems, noise, oversaturation, low intensity, or other
distortion. Police will instruct the victim to turn on the tape recorder
any time the telephone rings, prior to answering. Then if it is a
normal call the recorder can be turned off or the tape can be erased.
If the call is made by the criminal, the entire conversation should
be recorded.
  Some actual cases in which recordings of criminal calls were
obtained in this manner are:

U.S. v. *Moses Brown*, Superior Ct., District of Columbia, Wash-
    ington, D.C. (1973)
Commonwealth v. *Edward Lykus*, Superior Ct., New Bedford, MA.
    (1973)
U.S. v. *Earl F. Brown, Jr.*, U.S. District Ct., Eastern District of
    TN., No. 13130 (1974)
Michigan v. *Larry Nelson*, Circuit Ct., County of Oakland, MI.
    (1975)

Recordings of the voice of a suspected criminal can also be obtained by an undercover agent or informer using a body tape recorder or a transmitter. Usually this type of recording is noisy and of a poor quality. Bars and public places are the usual environments where the agent or informer goes to meet the suspected criminal in an attempt to record a self-incriminating conversation. An actual case where this manner of recording was used is:

U.S. v. *Lucas,* Southern District Federal Court, NY. (1974)

EXEMPLAR RECORDINGS OF KNOWN PERSONS (SUSPECTS OR DEFENDANTS)

To produce these recordings, an accurate transcript of the text of the criminal call should first be made. The interrogator who obtains these recordings should become familiar with the the transcript and the rate and aural characteristics of the criminal's voice prior to obtaining samples from the known persons. Then a recording system should be set up, including a telephone line if the recording of the criminal call was obtained through the telephone. (For those recordings not obtained through a telephone, exemplar recordings may be made with the suspect or defendant speaking directly into the tape recorder.) The telephone line should be as similar as possible to the one used by the criminal if some knowledge of its type is available. At the end of the telephone line where the interrogator sits, a tape recorder should be connected to that telephone. The telephone at the other end of the line is used by the defendant or the suspect. The system should be tested prior to the actual recording of known samples. When all the people involved are ready, and communication is established between the two ends of the telephone line, the interrogator states the date, time, place, his name, and the name of the defendant or suspect being recorded. Then the interrogator asks the defendant or suspect to utter the first sentence of the transcript of the criminal call, saying, for example: "Please, Mr. X, repeat after me: I will plant a bomb." The defendant or suspect repeats this sentence. If the interrogator is not satisfied for any reason, due to errors or apparent marked deviations from the natural rate, pitch, or articulation of the defendant's speech, he must ask the defendant or suspect to repeat the sentence as many times as necessary. The recording now continues with the second sentence, in the same manner as with the first one, until the whole content of the transcript is completed.

The entire procedure can be repeated several times. In addition, a direct tape recording can be obtained at the same time from the defendant or suspect, because these can sometimes be helpful to the voice identification examiner. Proper placement, an adequate type of microphone, and a reasonably quiet environment are required for such recordings of the known voices. The microphone should be undirectional, placed about 30 cm from the mouth of the defendant at an approximate angle of 70°. The recording system should ensure a frequency response the same as or better than the telephone line. If particular areas of resonance due to environment or recording system are known or detected, they should be corrected when this is possible, or information on this particular matter should be provided to the voice identification examiner.

Recordings should be played back before the defendant or suspect leaves so that the officer in charge may correct any deficiency of the samples. Collaboration of the defendant or suspect is crucial to obtain these samples and should be ensured by court order if necessary (see U.S. Supreme Court decision on *U.S.* v. *Dionisio* (1973)).

Both the criminal call and the samples must be properly rerecorded for use as exemplars through patch wires using well maintained and tested tape recorders connected to power outlets. Open reel or cassette tapes used to record these exemplars should be of a good quality and clean. Bias voltage of the tape recorders utilized should be properly adjusted to the characteristics of the magnetic tape used. Tapes should be properly labeled regarding content and mailed or delivered to the voice identification examiner to ensure that the chain of custody is not broken. The examiner should also be careful to protect the chain of custody as required by law—to initial all materials received and to keep a record with dates and events concerning the case.

PREPARATION OF AURAL MATERIALS
AND SPECTROGRAMS FOR EXAMINATION

Prior to preparing aural materials and spectrograms for the voice examination, the examiner should listen carefully to the recordings received and check the transcripts to detect any discrepancy with the spoken text. If the examiner did not receive a transcript of the text of the criminal call, he should prepare one.

The exemplar tapes, especially the one containing the criminal call, could be submitted to filtering to enhance some particular range of frequencies, and to temporally segment the portions containing the interlocutor voice if the criminal call consisted of a dialog between two persons, only one of whom is the criminal or the person under investigation.

These exemplars should also be dubbed into master open reel magnetic tapes of 1.5 mill thickness, recorded at 7.5 ips on one track. These master tapes will be actually used to obtain spectrograms and materials for aural examinations.

Preparation of Spectrograms

The examiner starts by placing the master tape containing the criminal call in the spectrograph. The first 2.4-sec segment to be analyzed is fixed in the rotating head loop drum by listening to it through the spectrograph monitor loudspeaker or headphones connected to the playback system of the instrument.

Settings of the spectrograph for voice identification purposes usually are: broadband spectrogram, linear expanded scale of 60–4,000 Hz, and high shaping (12 dB/octave amplification). A spectrogram of the 2.4-sec segment of speech recorded on the portion of tape clamped at the rotating head loop drum is produced and examined. Position of frequency marks of this spectrogram are checked with a standard template. If noise in particular bands is observed, attempts to filter it should be made if, of course, this filtering would not produce a loss of speech information. Also, particular bands of frequency may need to be amplified.

In addition to the high shaping spectrograms, another type using a flat shaping should be produced and compared with the previous one. The experience of the examiner will help him to find the best compromise setting to obtain the optimum spectrographic information. Some spectrograms with a scale of frequencies up to 7,000 Hz should be obtained also in case fricative information of those high bands is included in the recorded samples.

Subsequent 2.4-sec speech segments are processed in this fashion until the whole criminal call is completed. Immediately after each spectrogram is taken out of the machine it should be labeled "unknown"; the name of the case, the date, and the correlative number of the spectrogram should be specified using pen or pencil of a selected color at the superior edge of the paper. At the bottom of the spectrogram the portion of text represented should be written, targeting each word properly to the corresponding spectrographic patterns. A phonetic transcription or the normal spelling or both, one above the other, may be used for this purpose (see Figures 2.8 a, b, and c). Correct targeting is crucial; a professional examiner is expected to do a proper job concerning this matter. An electronic gate suggested by the author to the manufacturers of the spectrograph some years ago may help in some instances of difficult targeting. This gate allows the examiner to segment any short portion (a syllable or a word, for instance), by listening to it, from the 2.4-sec speech loop analyzed; the gate also permits the examiner to obtain the isolated spectrographic pattern of that short portion at exactly the same place it is situated in the whole spectrogram. Comparing these two spectrograms will help the examiner to properly target the spectrogram text.

Incidentally, at the Institute of Voice Identification of Michigan State University, the "gated" and the whole spectrograms are transferred from the instrument to a large monitor television set via a storage oscilloscope. Spectrograms appear together one above the other on the television screen. This method proved to be excellent for training students in this particular aspect of the technique.

Words portrayed on the spectrogram must be evaluated aurally; otherwise, there is a possibility of the examiner attempting a comparison between two different words from the unknown and known samples. If the analysis is done by using samples of a language unknown to the examiner, the services of an expert in that language are required to complete this step.

The author has faced a problem related to targeting when analyzing samples in Hebrew or Arabic. Although the phonetic transcription of these languages using the International Phonetic Alphabet can be done by writing from left to right, the experts in these languages expressed reluctance toward, and some technical difficulties with, that form of transliteration, preferring the normal one of those languages, that is, right to left. Consequently, the author has suggested the production of spectrographs with a reversed sense of rotation that can generate temporal spectrographic patterns from right to left for those examiners dealing mainly with languages customarily written in that sequence.

The master tapes of the known persons should be processed in the same manner; the corresponding spectrograms are to be labeled with the name or number of the related known speaker, the case, the date, and the correlative number of the spectrogram using a pen or pencil of a different color than the one used for the unknown spectrograms. Also, the text should be transcribed at the bottom of the spectrogram following same procedure as indicated for the unknown spectrograms.

Preparation of Aural Materials

A convenient way of arranging the unknown and known voices for comparison of perceptual features by using the short-term memory process is to dub the segments of the texts into continuous loop cartridges of 90-sec duration. Four tracks can be used in each cartridge. In each track a segment of 2 sec or so should be recorded as many times as the duration of the loop allows. The segment should correspond to a sentence or a grammatical unit to avoid cutting the melodic speech pattern of the speaker. Output from the spectrograph or a Cannon loop-recorder tape recorder may be used to simplify these recordings. Playing back each track allows the examiner to listen continuously and repeatedly to each 2-sec speech segment.

As many cartridges as necessary should be used to record in this manner the complete text from the unknown and known voices. Cartridges must be properly labeled and numbered correlatively in such a manner that track n of cartridge m from the unknown talker contains the same sentence as track n of cartridge m of the known talkers' samples. Two cartridge tape recorders should be connected to a two-channel amplifier, outputting them to a couple of loudspeakers or to earphones. A suitable system of switches should allow the examiner to select alternatively and quickly any of the corresponding unknown and known segments to be compared aurally. Recording levels of all these loops should be adjusted to the same overall volume.

EXAMINATION OF VOICES

With these materials—magnetic tape loops and spectrograms from the unknown and known voices—the examiner proceeds with the examination of voices for purposes of identification or elimination.

Aural Examination of Recordings

The examiner puts the 90-sec loop cartridges containing the same sentences from the unknown and one of the known voices into the two tape recorders that are connected to the two-channel amplifier. He plays back and listens alternately to both voices, repeating the same sentence as often and as long as he deems necessary. The loop arrangement of the cartridges facilitates such continuous listening. The examiner listens critically, comparing perceptual features from the two voices, such as melody pattern, pitch, quality, respiratory group, and any peculiar observable common feature that may be noticed. For instance, in the case of *U.S.* v. *Brown* (1973), speech samples from both the unknown talker and the defendant included a peculiar whistling at the end of some sentences, which served as a strong clue for positive identification. In many cases a difference in pitch is observed between the unknown voice and the known voice; the unknown recording often presents a higher pitch than that in the known recording. In this case a good practice is to alter the pitches from either recording, using the "Varimax" tape recorder, for instance, to bring them to equality. This procedure eliminates one variable that is not a comparable feature while not interfering too much with those variables that are to be compared (within some limits, of course). In addition, in most cases a more precise articulation and a slower rhythm is observed in the known voice samples than in the unknown one. A trained examiner expects to find these differences and can recognize that usual range of intratalker variation through experience acquired during the examination of a considerable number of cases.

When there is more than one known voice, the procedure is repeated comparing each of these suspected voices with the unknown one. Sometimes comparisons are done also among several unknown voices to determine whether or not they belong to the same person.

The examiner may reach a tentative decision of identification or elimination after this aural examination is completed. Spectrographic examination migh confirm or refute this tentative decision. Eventually a panel of listeners may also be utilized to judge similarities or dissimilarities of the compared voices.

Visual Examination of Spectrograms

After sets of spectrograms from the unknown and known voices are prepared as previously explained, the matching task to detect their spectrographic similarities or differences starts. The examiner places pairs of spectrograms showing the same sentences side by side and compares them word for word. There are guiding clues for matching considered by every examiner, such as similarity of mean frequencies, bandwidths, and slopes of vowels formants; interformants; fricative, plosive, and nasal power density pattern distributions; duration of plosive gaps; and peculiar spectrographic "gestalt." Of course, a trained examiner has to disregard characteristic phonetic similarities in the same way that a trained handwriting expert ignores the common characteristics of each letter of the alphabet when comparing an unknown handwriting sample with a known one for purposes of identification or elimination.

Peculiar acoustic density distribution patterns are very important clues for spectrographic identification if found at the same frequency/time coordinates in the unknown and one of the known sample spectrograms. For instance, in one criminal case a characteristic isolated spike was found in both the unknown and the known sample spectrograms of the word "mad" below the second formant at the midpoint of the duration of this word (Figure 4.1). This peculiar type of similarity gives substantial weight toward a positive identification. Indeed the chances that such a peculiar spike of energy at those precise coordinates of a word could be produced by different persons are very remote, in the opinion of the author.

An examiner never expects to find two spectrograms so similar that they can be overlapped. This is also the case in most systems of identification, including handwriting analysis, fingerprinting, ballistics, etc.

Dissimilarities found in both unknown and known sets of spectrograms can be attributed to intratalker or intertalker differences. For instance, some difference in pitch or coarticulation due to slight phonetic variations may alter the mean frequencies of formants in spectrograms of similar sentences produced by the same person as well as those produced by different persons. The experience and subjective judgment of a professional examiner determines whether these differences are due to intratalker or intertalker variability, leading to identification or elimination respectively. Only in cases beyond doubt, subjectively speaking, is the examiner entitled to make a positive identification. In all other instances he should indicate a probability of identification or of elimination, or no opinion one way or the other.

The basic controversy in the system is over where the divisory

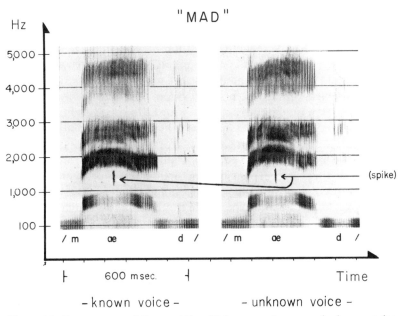

Figure 4.1. Spectrograms of the word "mad" from an unknown and a known voice. Observe the characteristic power spike at approximately the same frequency/time coordinates in both spectrograms.

line between inter- and intratalker differences should be plotted. In the opinion of the author, this judgment must be made by experienced professional examiners of spectrograms who have spent a number of years performing this job. A general speech scientist, with no special training in voice identification by use of spectrograms, can hardly give an opinion on this subject no matter how excellent are his credentials in speech sciences.

   Observation of trainees' performances over a reasonable period has convinced the author that indeed actual practice is the main factor responsible for correct matchings of spectrograms. However, this statement can be proven only through experimentation including that variable. The relatively small study by Smrkovski (1976) did suggest it is true. Presently, a larger experiment in which spectrograms are examined by professional examiners qualified by the International Association of Voice Identification and by novices with little training is in progress. The author expects to report that experiment within a few months.

   Statistical data obtained from this and other controlled experiments can be used to plot the receiver operating characteristic of each trainee at given intervals of time. This recommended procedure might produce a reliable indication of the influence or lack of influence of experience on correct matching of spectrograms.

It should again be pointed out that most reported experiments on the spectrographic method of voice identification were performed by experimental examiners with little or no training at all. Results of these experiments can be taken only as a relative measure, hardly applicable to practical performance of professional examiners with at least two years of practical experience in the field who know they are responsible for presentation of evidence that can help to convict or acquit the defendant.

A psychophysical ranking scale to quantify the similarities and differences subjectively obtained by an examiner is presently being experimented with by the author. Essentially, this scale consists of 20 rankings: 10 to 0 for great to little similarity and 0 to -10 for little to great difference. The procedure to follow is very simple: each pair of words from the unknown and known sample spectrograms are compared and by subjective decision a number from the scale is chosen to express the similarity or dissimilarity between the pair. After the examiner has ranked all pairs of similar words from the unknown and known samples, the average ranking number is computed. This figure, or a suitable monotonic transformation such as $2 \sin^{-1} \sqrt{x}$, can be used as a base for reaching the final decision on whether the samples were produced by the same or by different persons.

This procedure has the advantages of: 1) considering similarities as well as dissimilarities between samples; 2) being largely independent of the sample length; 3) disclosing clearly the process followed to reach the final conclusion; and 4) homogenizing examiners' criteria for testing their reliability. It should be pointed out that this procedure was adopted after the author received some criticisms from his colleagues, such as: "dissimilarities of samples are disregarded, thus assuming they have been originated by intraspeaker differences;" "given a long enough sample, it is always possible to find a minimum number of similarities to produce a positive identification;" and "the technique is esoteric—nobody, including the court and the jury, can possibly understand what the examiner did." The author hopes this procedure will be acceptable to concerned speech scientists.

The author has given several voice identification cases to some of his trainees to be examined using the psychophysical ranking scale discussed. In each case the average ranking numbers yielded by each of these trainees were the same to the tenths.

In most instances the scale has proved to be discriminative enough with controlled data. However, the author realizes that there could be voices very similar to each other for which the scale would not discriminate sufficiently. For these cases a special algorithm could be applied to particular regions of the scale to amplify the grade of discrimination. Experimentation is being conducted on this aspect.

To further illustrate the application of the suggested psychophysical ranking scale to quantify similarities and differences between spectrograms, three sets of them, A–B/A–C; D–E/D–F; and G–H/G–I, will here be compared word for word. It should be understood that these are not examples of complete voice identification examinations but only short examples illustrating this procedure as utilized to match spectrograms in the visual phase of the examination.

Example A–B/A–C (Figure 4.2)

Word	Ranking, spectrograms A and B	Comments
I	−7	1st formants are quite similar; slopes of 3rd formants are completely different; 4th formant does not exist in B
got	−5	Duration is different; plosive spikes, slopes and patterns, 2nd formants, interformant separation quite different
five	−9	2nd and 3rd formant slopes, interformant separation completely different
grands	−7	All formants present quite different patterns and mean frequencies

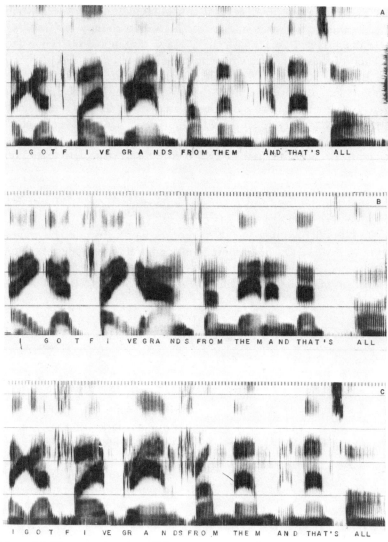

Figure 4.2. Three spectrograms of the same sentence. Spectrogram A represents an unknown voice; spectrograms B and C represent known voices.

from	−7	Fricative patterns, 2nd and 3rd formant slopes width of 3rd formants very different
them	−5	Mean frequencies and separation formants different; nasal patterning different
and	−8	Quite different patterns and slopes of formants
that's	−6	2nd and 3rd formants differ but 1st and 4th present some similarity; fricative quite different
all	2	There are some differences in slopes, but this is due to differences in intonation as checked in aural examination

Average ranking number between spectrograms A and B = −5.78.

Word	Ranking, spectro-grams A and C	Comments
I	8	Separation and beginnings of 2nd and 3rd formants, some difference; other patterns very similar
got	8	Some minor differences observed in 2nd and 4th formants
five	8	Small difference in fricative and endings of 2nd and 3rd formants
grands	9	The patterns can almost overlap
from	9	All features quite similar
them	8	All features but duration are very similar
and	2	Mean frequency, 2nd formants, and slopes differ; initial transients differ but

		there is a very similar spike at that position
that's	9	They could almost overlap
all	9	Same comment

Average ranking number between spectrograms A and C = 7.78

Conclusion High level of confidence that spectrograms A and C correspond to the same talker and about 75% to 80% probability that spectrograms A and B correspond to different talkers.

Example D–E/D–F (Figure 4.3)

Word	Ranking, spectrograms D and E	Comments
Did	8	Except for duration all features are quite similar
you	9	Observe the striking similarities of slopes and power distribution of formants
see	8	All features very close
Johnny	9	Same comment
last	9	Practically no difference
week	9	"Overlapping" features

Average ranking number between spectrograms D and E = 8.67

Word	Ranking, spectrograms D and F	Comments
Did	−9	Almost everything, except 1st and 4th formants, is quite different
you	−7	Different formant slopes and structures
see	−6	Differences in dynamics of formants
Johnny	−7	3rd formants differ markedly
last	4	Dynamics of formants differ, but mean frequency coincides
week	−9	Patterns differ in nearly all aspects

Average ranking number spectrograms D and F = −5.67

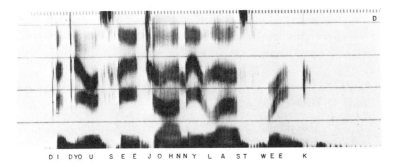

DI DYO U   S E E   J O H N N Y   L A   S T   W E E   K

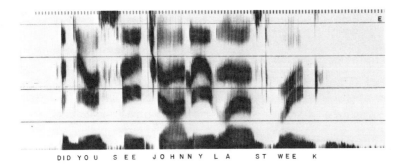

DID YO U   S EE   J O H N N Y   L A   S T   W E E   K

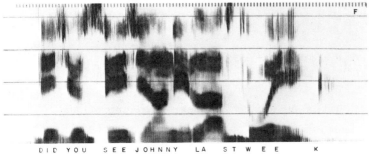

DI D YO U   S E E JOHNNY   L A   S T W E E   K

Figure 4.3. Three spectrograms of the same sentence. Spectrogram D represents an unknown voice; spectrograms E and F represent known voices.

Conclusion High degree of confidence that spectrograms D and E correspond to the same talker and about 70% to 75% probability that spectrograms D and F correspond to different talkers.

Example G–H/G–I (Figure 4.4)

Word	Ranking, spectrograms G and H	Comments
I	−6	3rd formants differ; some similarity is found between 2nd and 3rd formants
will	−4	Spectrographic patterns too weak
wait	−9	Quite different slopes; different power density distribution
for	2	Some similarity of fricative and final transients is considered
you	−6	Mean frequencies differ; 3rd formants are quite different
at	2	Some similarity is considered
the	2	Same comment
bus	−7	2nd formant's dynamic quite different
station	−9	Slopes of 2nd formants as well as affricative power distributions differ markedly

Average ranking number between spectrograms G and H = −3.89

Word	Ranking, spectrograms G and I	Comments
I	−4	Mean frequencies and formant structures different
will	−10	Completely different
wait	−7	Substantial differences in formant characteristics

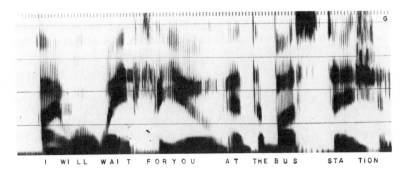

I   WI LL   WA I T   F O R Y O U   A T   THE B U S   STA   TION

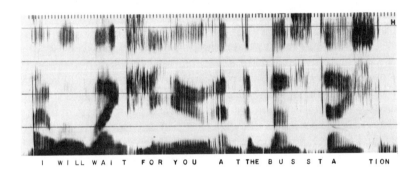

I   W I LL WA I T   FOR   Y O U   A   T THE B U S   S T A   T I ON

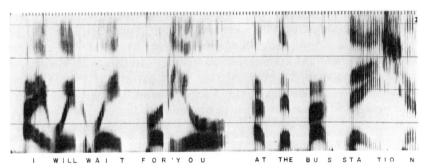

I   WILL WA I T   F O R ' Y O U   AT   THE   BU   S   STA   T I O   N

Figure 4.4. Three spectrograms of the same sentence. Spectrogram G represents an unknown voice; spectrograms H and I represent known voices.

for	−10	No relation between the two utterances
you	−10	Completely different slopes
at	−7	Differences in 4th formants
the	−7	Same comment
bus	−8	Different formants and slopes
station	−9	Same comment

Average ranking number between spectrograms G and I = −8.00

Conclusion   High level of confidence that spectrograms G and I were produced by different talkers and about 60 to 65% probability that spectrograms G and H were produced by different talkers.

Of course, these average ranking numbers between two pairs of samples only rank them according to degree of probability that they are from the same or from different talkers if one unknown is compared with two or more knowns, as in the illustrations presented. If only one known talker sample is compared with the unknown one, the decision criterion will have to be based on only the single available average ranking number. Testing this suggested scale with controlled data might bring valid information on the correct way to interpolate the average ranking number within the final decision criterion (especially helpful in single comparison cases). (As a further example, the reader is invited to rank spectrogram 1 as compared with spectrograms A, B, and C in Figure 4.5.)

In addition to comparing spectrograms to complete the voice identification examination, the examiner again listens to the voices while simultaneously examining the spectrograms before producing his opinion. In this last phase of the simultaneous examination, he may detect differences in pitch, phonetic variations, etc., between the aural samples that might explain some corresponding spectrographic differences.

An examination may be completed in whatever amount of time the examiner deems sufficient. The examination may not necessarily be concluded during a single session but could be interrupted if in the judgment of the examiner this option is needed to overcome tiredness or boredom.

A good practice for examiners is to request an opinion from a colleague, providing him with the samples used but without disclosing to him any opinion concerning them. The author, Lt.

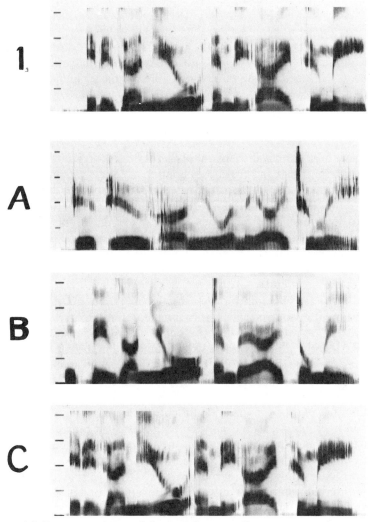

Figure 4.5. Four spectrograms of the same sentence. Spectrogram 1 represents an unknown voice; spectrograms A, B, and C represent known voices. Compare 1 with A, B, and C.

Smrkovski, and Mr. Lundgren very often follow this procedure. These three examiners have thus far agreed with each other's conclusions, very often basing their conclusions on the same decision criterion but, of course, with no previous knowledge of which criterion was used by the one responsible for the examination.

COURTROOM DIRECT AND CROSS-EXAMINATION

Through all the legal cases involving voice identification, a typical pattern for direct and cross-examination of expert witnesses in voice identification has developed. Its description may help district attorneys and defense counselors, as a general suggestion only, to prepare their own trial strategies in the event they should deal with this type of evidence. In this description it is assumed that the voice of the defendant has been positively identified by a professional examiner as being the same as that of the unknown person. Therefore, the prosecuting district attorney takes the direct examination and the defense counselor the cross-examination of the prosecution expert witnesses and vice versa for the defense expert witnesses.

In the pretrial hearing, the court must decide whether or not voice identification evidence will be accepted in the subsequent jury trial. The hearing normally begins with direct examination of the prosecution expert witness by the prosecutor. After the usual questions to identify the examiner, an attempt is made to restrict the field of expertise on voice identification to only those who practice it on a professional and continuous basis. The reason is that frequently the expert witness for the defense is a general speech scientist rather than a professional examiner, and prosecutors seek to disqualify these adversary witnesses. The Frye rule[1] comes under consideration here. The criteria for accepting or not accepting the Frye rule as applied to the whole community of speech scientists or to the restricted field of voice identification examiners have varied according to each court involved. The prosecutor then offers his witness to the court as an expert witness in the field of voice identification. Usually the defense does not attempt to disqualify this expert witness if he has really proven he is working in the field

---

[1] *Frye* v. *U.S.* (1923), in which a decision of the U.S. Supreme Court rules that evidence could not be presented in that trial because "the relevant scientific community generally does not accept such a method." This ruling is frequently used in an attempt to disqualify evidence generated by voice identification methods on the same grounds.

and has a reasonable background in speech sciences. However, in addition to the testimony of a practitioner proper foundation of the method used by a scientist is absolutely necessary in most cases (cf. *California* v. *Kelly*, 1973). The direct examination continues with a description of voice identification methods and spectrography. In particular, the Tosi et al. (1972) experiment, currently the best evidence for the validity of voice identification, is described in detail.

At this point, cross-examination takes place. The defense counselor tries to discredit favorable extrapolations from laboratory experiments to practical cases of voice identification, arguing that the many different factors encountered in real life, as opposed to laboratory experiments, render such extrapolations inapplicable to actual legal cases. In redirect this argument is debated by stating that all conditions that may produce differences in the spectrograms between the unknown and known voices may lead only to a no-opinion decision, or at the worst to a false elimination, rather than to a false identification; these alternatives are generally acceptable within our philosophy of justice. Only when the examiner is convinced beyond reasonable doubt that the unknown sample and the defendant's sample belong to the same person will he make a positive, or highly confident, identification. In other cases he abstains from giving an opinion one way or the other, makes a positive elimination (correctly or incorrectly), or states only probabilities.

At this time the defense counselor puts his expert witness on the stand and tries to qualify him through the usual questions. In the cross-examination, the prosecutor presses this witness by questioning him about the experience he has specifically in voice identification, rather than in speech and hearing sciences in general. Many well-recognized scientists brought to court by subpoena or appearing of their own volition have failed to qualify as experts in voice identification, some of them by their own admission, due to lack of actual practice in this field. This point should be considered by the defense lawyers. Rather than attacking the method as an invalid one by using general speech scientists, they may consider the option of securing a professional examiner who might testify on behalf of the defendant, if such an examiner has found only a probability of identification or elimination or has no opinion one way or the other after examination of the evidence. However, if the prosecution's expert witness has reached a positive, or highly confident, identification it is rather unlikely that two qualified examiners could arrive at different conclusions. Nevertheless the defense may want to consider such an option over an attempt to discredit voice identification.

The defense counselor, through questioning his expert witness, continues with arguments to discredit voice identification by aural and spectrographic examination of speech samples. One tactic is to declare that the only basis for accepting this method is the Tosi et al. (1972) experiment and that this experiment's conclusions cannot be applied to practical cases. For instance, one expert witness for the defense stated repeatedly that the number of tests in that experiment, in relation to the variables involved in the legal case on trial, were too few to draw conclusions of any significance. The trial variables under discussion were: noncontemporary spectrograms, connected speech, telephone line transmission, and only one examiner involved (cf. *Massachusetts* v. *Lykus,* 1973). That expert witness considered these conditions to be represented by only 12 tests among the 34,996 tests included in the Tosi et al. experiment. In cross-examination the prosecutor attempted to establish whether or not that expert witness had properly read the report of the experiment, after demonstrating with simple facts that his figures were wrong (he has changed the actual number from case to case). In a subsequent case, after hearing a similar argument and cross-examination of the same person, the judge decided that that witness "can't keep his numbers straight between 5 and 20,000" (cf. *U.S.* v. *Brown,* 1973). The same antagonistic expert witness indicated that the method of voice identification by aural and spectrographic examination of speech samples is completely unreliable, while admitting on the other hand that on about five occasions he has made voice eliminations by using the aural short-term memory process, which is part of that method, as explained before (cf. *N.Y.* v. *Barnes,* 1977). Defense counselors should watch for these types of wrong statements or contradictions that an extremist opponent can make, which will have obvious bad effects on the defendant's case.

Other experts have testified that there are many other experiments that contradict the results from the Tosi et al. (1972) experiment and that, therefore, results from that study should not be considered valid. In cross-examination this argument is debated by questioning the statistical significance of experiments including only 400 tests as compared with the extent of the Tosi et al. study. Also, the different approaches taken in these studies that seem to contradict the results from Tosi et al. are brought out in cross-examination. Sometimes these arguments are reinforced by introducing letters such as the one from Dr. K. Stevens to Prosecutor Lindhom (1971) or from Dr. Peter Ladefoged to Dr. David (1971). Very often the paper by Bolt et al. (1973) is introduced by the defense in an effort to disqualify the method. In redirect the paper by Black et al. (1973) is then introduced by the prosecution as a favorable exhibit toward the validity of the method.

At this point the court decides whether or not it will allow the voice identification evidence to be introduced in the actual jury trial. Up to the present it has been accepted in all cases except that of *California* v. *Chapter* (1973), in which the court rejected the voice identification testimony on the grounds that it does not comply with the Frye rule and that in addition the voice identification examiner had committed several errors. Once voice identification evidence is accepted in the hearing, the same preliminary process of explaining the method takes place during jury trial. Then spectrograms and magnetic tapes including the unknown sample and the defendant's voice sample are introduced as exhibits. These exhibits include, very often, a magnetic tape recording containing sequences of the unknown voice and the defendant's voice uttering the same sentences, which is played back to the jury.

Similarities from both sets of spectrograms are shown and explained to the court and the jury if the defense insists on this procedure. It is preferable to avoid doing so because if this is done, each member of the jury might feel like becoming an instant expert in matching spectrographic similarities, which could be fatal for the prosecution.

The defense, in response to the show of similarity, could present spectrograms and magnetic tapes of the same text as that of the criminal call produced by a person with a voice with the same general characteristics as the defendant's voice (thus very probably showing a close match to that of the unknown voice). These materials could then be used to convince a jury of the difficulty or probability of error when identifying a person through his/her voice. Another resource the defense may have is to demand that the receiver operating characteristic of the prosecutor's expert witness be produced and entered as evidence and to request that this examiner be given an open test, including the voice of the defendant among the voices of other people and identifying the voices by a number rather than by a name.

Finally, it should be noted that in most trials, visual materials presented through an overhead projector were used to explain the process involved in voice identification by spectrography. Actual spectrograms from the case are not shown in that manner because of technical problems with photocopying transparencies.

TRAINING OF VOICE IDENTIFICATION EXAMINERS

There are two institutions that offer training for voice identification examiners using aural and spectrographic examination of speech samples. One of these is the Michigan State University Institute of Voice Identification, which offers periodic workshops of 1 month duration, full time (eight hours a day), taught jointly with the crime laboratory of the Michigan Department of State Police. This workshop includes both theoretical and practical training in voice identification by aural and spectrographic examination of speech samples and explanations of other methods. The theoretical training consists of lectures on acoustic phonetics, theory of voice production, and speech spectrography. Practical training consists of aural examination of voices and visual examination of spectrograms of voices using laboratory and practical case samples.

The level of the lectures on acoustic phonetics and voice production is adjusted to the average type of student attending each workshop; usually it is given at an elementary level. General characteristics of sound, simple harmonic motion, representation of waves in the temporal and in the frequency domain, complex waves, Fourier analysis, resonances, production of speech, acoustic characteristics of speech sounds, and coarticulation phenomena are discussed at length. Lectures also provide a rather comprehensive discussion on phonetics and a practicum on the usage of the International Phonetic Alphabet.

The practical training of workshop students starts with very simple cases of voice identification using closed trials and contemporary spectrograms. Explanations of which kind of similarity patterns should be detected in order to properly identify an unknown voice as one of several known voices are offered to the students using suitable samples. Rating scales are thoroughly discussed. Training continues with more complicated cases involving noncontemporary spectrograms and open trials until the students reach a criterion of at least 90% correct answers. Then more complicated cases are offered, including noisy samples and samples of very similar voices. Also, aural examinations are practiced and discussed with examples. Aural tests are given to the students according to a graduated degree of difficulty, from very simple cases, with closed trials and contemporary recordings, to more complicated cases involving noncontemporary recordings, open trials, and, later on, recordings with noise.

Once the students have shown proficiency in handling combined aural and spectrographic examinations from laboratory cases, actual practical cases from the Voice Identification Unit of the Michigan Department of State Police are offered to them for examination. They are left on their own to perform the whole process, from original recordings to final results.

In addition, the students are coached in performing all laboratory dubbings, filterings, and segmentations of samples as discussed in the section on "Preparation of Spectrograms and Aural Materials for Examination." Instruction is provided on how to prepare a transcript, how to present the unknown voice text to a suspected person for recording satsifactory known voice samples, and how to obtain samples from known voices in an actual setting imitating a field situation.

A final examination, including a practical case, is given to the students, covering the theoretical and practical aspects of voice examinations.

This workshop on voice identification and elimination is offered to scientists, to crime laboratory technicians with good scientific background, and to lawyers. They are requested, prior to coming to the workshop, to study the subject or at least to be very familiar with the book by Denes and Pinson, *The Speech Chain* (1963). Up to the present this workshop has been attended by approximately 15 persons, including foreign personnel from Israel, South Africa, Japan, Canada, and Iran.

After the student successfully completes this workshop, he/she is advised to work at least 2 years in practical cases under the supervision of a member of the International Association of Voice Identification, if he/she desires to become a professional examiner. In addition, a curriculum to further complete theoretical studies is suggested to each student. These studies could be done at the student's home university.

It should be pointed out that the Michigan State University Institute of Voice Identification does not provide any certificate of professional competency in voice identification, but only a certificate of attendance of this workshop.

Another institution that provides a rather limited training on spectrography as applied to voice identification is Voiceprint, Inc., of New Jersey. That course has an approximate duration of 1 week; it deals with practical aspects of the spectrograph and with solving trials of identification using the original Kersta spectrograms.

chapter 5
LEGAL IMPLICATIONS OF VOICE IDENTIFICATION AND ELIMINATION

Up to the present only subjective methods of voice identification and elimination have been used as evidence in courts of law. Evidence based on the long-term memory aural process has been accepted since antiquity in most legal courts, taken from lay witnesses for what it was worth in each case, similar to the manner in which visual identification is accepted from any eyewitness.

The relatively recent introduction of the tape recorder together with the possibility of using the short-term memory aural process and, later on, the appearance of the acoustic spectrograph, have produced the voice identification expert witness in the court of law. Consequently, a very emotional controversy on the issue has taken place. Some scientists insist that subjective methods of voice identification are not valid for use in a court of law (Bolt et al., 1973); others claim that within some limits they are (Black et al., 1973); in both camps there are extremists (Hollien, 1977; Truby, 1977) and moderates (Rothman, 1977; Tosi, 1977). The problem is further complicated by two facts: (1) many expert witnesses of voice identification are practitioners who sometimes differ with the scientific modality, exacerbating the conflict; and (2) available laboratory experimentation on subjective methods of voice identification cannot completely clarify the conflict because their results are difficult to compare and extrapolations to practical conditions are not consistent because they depend on particular points of view and experiences.

Courts also differ in their acceptance of subjective methods of voice identification. In approximately 85 cases tried since 1971, these methods have been accepted, but there were also some reversals on the grounds that the aural and spectrographic examination of speech samples "does not satisfy the Frye rule"—in other words, that "the relevant scientific community generally does not accept such a method." Because the problem here is to define what *is* the scientific community relevant to voice identification, legal opinions are divided. The two opposite points of view of legal practitioners were expressed, among others, by Jones (1973, 1974), a defense counselor who adamantly opposes voice identification by spectrograms, and by Greene (1975), a federal prosecutor who strongly advocates its usage. A federal judge, the Hon. Timothy Murphy, is a defender of spectrography (Murphy, 1977); another judge, the Hon. Paul Barker, is convinced that this method should not be used in a court of law but left for investigative purposes only (Barker, 1977).

In 1976 the FBI requested the National Academy of Sciences to study the problem and to provide recommendations concerning the validity of aural and spectrographic examination of speech samples for voice identification. The National Academy of Sciences then assembled a special committee of scientists to perform such a study and to produce the recommendations requested. Dr. Richard Bolt was elected chairman of that committee, which is composed of 8 members, including this author. The committee has been working from November 1976 to the present. The task of the Committee on Speech Spectrograms of the National Academy of Sciences did not involve any experimental work; it consisted of discussions among the members, evaluations of existing literature in the subject, and hearings granted to all parties interested. Its final report is due in March or April 1978, and no doubt its recommendations will be received with interest by all parties concerned with the problem of voice identification.

LEGALITY OF VOICE IDENTIFICATION BEFORE DECEMBER 1970

The first attempt to introduce an expert witness on voice identification in a court of law was made by Lawrence Kersta in 1966 *State* v. *Rispoli and Straehle,* 1966). Kersta, a former scientist from Bell Telephone Laboratories, retired in 1962 and organized his own firm, Voiceprint Laboratories, Inc., in New Jersey. The purposes of that corporation were to commercially produce the spectrograph in competition with Kay Elemetrics Co., to offer professional services in voice identification, and to train law enforcement officers to operate the spectrograph for voice identification purposes. It is to be noted that Kersta did not use the short-term memory aural examination of voices for identification but only visual examination of spectrograms. Training consisted of attending Kersta's sessions at the Laboratory for approximately 10 days and subsequently continuing examinations of spectrograms during a period of 2 years, under Kersta's supervision. About 20 persons attended these sessions and only a few completed the training. The first class was offered in 1967; it was attended by Lt. Ernest Nash, by another officer from the crime laboratory of Michigan Department of State Police, and by the author, as a consultant to that police department, with the purpose of evaluating Kersta's procedures.

Voiceprint Laboratories, Inc., went into bankruptcy in 1973. In total, Kersta presented legal evidence in only eight cases. (A list of these cases is presented in Appendix A.) One of the last cases in which Kersta acted as an expert witness was *California* v. *King* (1968). This case was related to the Watts (a section of Los Angeles) riots of 1966, and involved arson and looting. During a television interview, a young man, not showing his face to the camera, bragged of being the one responsible for the arson. Los Angeles police were unable to obtain the name of that person from the broadcast, but through informers a suspected individual was held in custody. Kersta was called by the authorities to decide whether or not the voice recorded by the television station was the same as that of the suspected person, Mr. King. Kersta made spectrograms from the unknown voice and from Mr. King's voice samples and decided that indeed both voices belonged to the same person. King was brought to trial, and Kersta acted as expert witness on behalf of the prosecution. Expert witness for the defense was Dr. Peter Ladefoged, who had been very adamantly opposed since the inception of the "voiceprinting" method to Kersta's claims of validity of voice identification by speech spectrograms (Ladefoged and Vanderslice, 1967). In that trial Ladefoged challenged very successfully the "voiceprinting" method as well as the credentials of Kersta in speech sciences. The defendant was acquitted by an appellate court.

In the case *New Jersey* v. *Cary* (1968) Kersta testified in favor of exclusive use of speech spectrograms for voice identification (aural examination was ignored by Kersta). Tosi also testified in that case, suggesting to the court that more experimentation was necessary prior to endorsing or rejecting the method. The New Jersey Supreme Court ruled accordingly; therefore, the spectrographic evidence was not accepted at that time. Subsequently, after the experiment on voice identification by Tosi et al. (1972) was completed, the New Jersey Supreme Court reversed its decision on spectrographic evidence and held that a defendant (*New Jersey* v. *Andretta,* 1972) would be required to give a voice sample for purposes of identification.

In total, Kersta and the staff of Voiceprint Laboratories performed voice identification examinations (using speech spectrograms exclusively) for approximately 200 clients.[1] After the bankruptcy of Voiceprint Laboratories, Inc., William Hughes bought its assets, funding the Voice Identification, Inc., company with the main purpose of continuing commercial production of the spectrograph. Because some of the personnel from Voiceprint Laboratories joined Voice Identification, Inc., this company also occasionally offers voice identification services similar to those offered by the former company.

One of the few cases in which evidence on voice identification by using only aural short-term memory was presented was *New Jersey* v. *DiGiglio* (1970). One expert witness for the defense in that case was the author who eliminated Mr. DiGiglio as being the same as the unknown person. Tosi was able to demonstrate in that case the different quality and pitch of the two voices examined, as well as the existence of a permanent hoarseness in the voice of Mr. DiGiglio due to chronic moncorditis that did not appear in the unknown voice.

Besides the United States, it seems that also in Russia some attempts at voice identification by examination of spectrograms were made (Solzhenitsyn, 1968). In South Africa, Dr. Len Jansen tried unsuccessfully to use spectrography to identify voices; according to his statements (*Michigan* v. *Nelson,* 1976), after attending the course on voice identification offered at the Institute of Voice Identification of Michigan State University he was able to perform the proper technique with reasonable success.

At the end of 1967, Tosi (1967) presented a report to the Michigan Department of State Police stating that:

> . . . after having evaluated the method called "Voiceprint" used by Kersta for voice identification purposes, I came to the opinion that the method shows promise, but before it could be endorsed or rejected it is necessary to perform an independent and comprehensive experimentation, including forensic models and variables not tested by Kersta.

---

[1] Information provided by Kersta to the author in a telephone conversation.

Such a study (Tosi et al., 1972) was performed at the Department of Audiology and Speech Sciences of Michigan State University from early 1968 to December 1970 with funds granted by the U.S. Department of Justice. At the same time, Lt. Ernest Nash of the crime laboratory at the Michigan Department of State Police was studying practical cases in order to compare spectrograms and general conditions of these cases with those existing at Tosi's laboratory. It was agreed that no material examined by Nash would be used as legal evidence during that period of experimentation.

During a period lasting about three years (1968 through 1970) there was no noticeable legal activity on voice identification.

LEGALITY OF VOICE IDENTIFICATION
FROM DECEMBER 1970 TO THE PRESENT

In December 1970, results from the Tosi and Nash studies became available, as reported in the section on "Visual Examination of Speech Spectrograms" in Chapter 3. As a consequence of this comprehensive experimentation and the experience gained with practical cases, the Michigan Department of State Police decided to organize a voice identification unit, headed by Lt. Nash, offering voice identification evidence in Michigan and elsewhere. It was agreed also that examinations must comply with the guidelines as discussed in the section on "Visual Examination of Speech Spectrograms."

The first time that voice identification evidence was handled in this manner, using a combined aural and spectrographic examination of speech samples, was in the case *Minnesota* v. *Trimble* (1970). The case concerned an anonymous telephone call to the police headquarters of St. Paul, Minnesota, from a girl requesting transportation to a hospital for her pregnant sister. Police sent a car to transport the alleged patient. The officer in charge was ambushed and killed when he arrived at the address given by the caller. St. Paul police investigated 13 suspected persons, obtaining samples of their voices. Twelve of these suspected persons were eliminated by Nash from consideration as being the same as the unknown caller, but Ms. Trimble was finally identified as such. The case was brought to trial. Dr. Peter Ladefoged acted as an expert witness for the defense; D/Lt. Nash and Dr. Tosi for the prosecution. During the course of that trial Dr. Ladefoged himself agreed with this identification, and finally Ms. Trimble confessed that she had indeed made the call by request of her boyfriend, although "she believed it to be only a joke." On these grounds she was acquitted by the jury. The Supreme Court of Minnesota decided in this case that spectrographic evidence was sufficient for the issuance of warrants.

As a consequence of his personal experience in this case, as well as the Tosi study and other factors, Dr. Ladefoged agreed at that point that in some cases it is possible to identify a person's voice by aural and spectrographic examination of speech samples.[2] Since that time Ladefoged has acted as an expert witness in cases involving voice identification by spectrography, either in favor (*U.S.* v. *Raymond,* 1971) or against it, according to the quality of the voice samples involved. This initial success, as well as the strong support of such prominent speech scientists as Dr. Henry Truby, Dr. John W. Black, and Dr. Karl Kryter, encouraged both the commanding officers of the Michigan State Police and the author to continue the use of speech spectrography for protecting the innocent (voice elimination) and indicting the criminal (voice identification).

The Voice Identification Unit of the Michigan Department of State Police was expanded with the incorporation of two new examiners, Detective Lonnie Smrkovski in 1971 and Detective Malcolm Hall in 1972. These two examiners were trained by Kersta and in addition they had completed studies in audiology and speech sciences at the Michigan State University in order to improve their expertise in this area. Smrkovsky received a bachelor's degree in Audiology and Speech Sciences in 1975 and Hall was granted a master's degree in that field in 1975, both under the direction of the author.

The Voice Identification Unit of the Michigan State Police completed approximately 4,000 voice sample examinations from December 1970 to June 1974, the time D/Lt. Nash left the Voice Identification Unit. About 65 cases were presented in court. Approximately 1,900 voice samples were eliminated from consideration as being the same as the unknown voice samples in the respective cases; for some 1,500 voice samples a no-opinion decision

---

[2] Dr. Lagefoged made these statements for the first time in a letter of 24 May 1971 addressed to Dr. Edward David, scientific adviser to the President of the United States. The last time the author heard the same statements by Dr. Lagefoged was at the December 1977 Florida meeting of the Academy of Forensic Applications of Communication Sciences (debate on "voiceprints").

was reached. The remaining voices examined yielded different degrees of probability.[3]

Nash was granted a leave of absence from the Michigan Department of State Police in June 1974; later on he retired to become a Representative in the Michigan State Legislature. Lt. Smrkovski replaced Nash as head of the Voice Identification Unit. In 1977 Nash also resigned as an active member of the International Association of Voice Identification.

The strong personality and absolute statements of Nash in the trials in which he acted as an expert witness produced strong reactions from the opponents as well as from some advocates of voice identification by spectrography. Drs. G. Papçun and P. Ladefoged (1973) presented a paper at the 86th meeting of the Acoustical Society of America, reviewing two cases examined by Nash and criticizing the quality of the samples used by this officer. Poza (1974) published a paper containing similar criticisms. In August 1973, in *California* v. *Chapter,* the court ruled that Nash had produced several errors in the voice examinations he performed for that case. In March 1973, in the case *Michigan* v. *Chaisson,* the court ordered Tosi to analyze the samples presented by Nash to the prosecutor as evidence against the defendant. Tosi reported that he was unable to use such samples for any kind of voice examination. However, he was able to offer a probability of identification on the basis of new samples obtained from the defendant, ordered by the court. The prosecution then dismissed that case.

At that moment there was consensus among many advocates of the method that all these circumstances had jeopardized the development of voice identification by aural and spectrographic examination of speech samples. Fortunately, all other practitioners have adopted a much more conservative position than the one shown by Lt. Nash.

Since December 1970 the number of professional voice identification examiners has grown, through the action of the International Association of Voice Identification (IAVI), up to approximately 18 members and 29 trainees (see Appendix B). The association has three categories of associates: members, trainees, and friends. Members are those persons who qualify through a 2-year apprenticeship in practical cases (under the supervision of a

---

[3] Data released by Lt. Nash to the writer.

member) and have passed a theoretical/practical examination provided by the Board of Directors; candidates with an advanced degree in Audiology and Speech Sciences are exempted from the theoretical examination, but they must pass the practical examination on voice identification to become a member. Trainees are those associates in the process of completing their 2-year apprenticeship by performing voice examinations from practical cases. Bylaws of the IAVI forbid them to offer testimony in a court of law during their apprenticeship. However, their supervisors, as members of IAVI, might act in the courtroom if necessary in a case with which the trainee was involved. There are no special requirements to become a friend of the association. The IAVI publishes a bulletin and organizes a yearly congress in different cities of the U.S. This association was created in May 1971 as a nonprofit corporation by L. Kersta, E. Nash, and O. Tosi; legal counselor for the association is Fredrich Stackable. Goals of the association are to monitor the training of prospective voice identification examiners (trainees) and to test them at the end of a minimum 2-year apprenticeship, to enforce a code of ethics, and to encourage research in voice identification by any method. There were only four examiner members of the association (due to a grandfather provision) at the time of its foundation—the three founders and Dr. Ladefoged.

Some prominent speech scientists, such as Drs. Karl Kryter, Herbert Oyer, and John W. Black, were appointed honorary members of the association. Present chairman of the Board of Directors is Dr. Henry Truby; the 1977–1978 President is Detective Malcolm Hall. In 1971 the House of Representatives and the Senate of Michigan issued Resolution #142 commemorating the incorporation of the International Association of Voice Identification and commending the goals set by its bylaws.

Professional examiners certified by the IAVI have offered voice identification evidence up to the present in approximately 80 trials in 23 state and federal courts, and in Canadian courts. In most cases these examiners acted for the prosecution, but there were also instances in which they acted on behalf of the defense, eliminating the defendant as being the same as the unknown caller (cf. *U.S.* v. *Sisco; Florida* v. *Otero,* etc.). The verdicts from all these trials varied; in about 46 cases (since December 1970) the defendants were found guilty, in 19 cases the defendants were acquitted; in 4 cases there were hung juries; in 8 cases the defendants pleaded guilty. In the remaining instances the cases were dismissed for different reasons. In approximately 25% of the cases there were adversary expert witnesses; these cases resulted in approximately 58% convictions. Notice that this percentage is not too far from the 61% of convictions obtained in all cases, since December 1970, whether or not adversary expert witnesses were present. A list of cases in which voice identification evidence was used is offered in Appendix A.

As of the beginning of 1978, voice identification by aural and spectrographic examination of speech samples has been accepted by federal courts and state courts of 23 states, as well as in Canada, Italy, and Israel. There were several reversals and upholdings by appellate courts (see Appendix A), and three reversals and three upholdings by state supreme courts in California, Pennsylvania, Minnesota, Massachusetts, and New Jersey.

In the reversal of the State Supreme Court of California concerned the case *California* v. *Kelly* (1976), the court's ruling does not preclude the usage of voice identification by speech spectrograms in California. Reversal of the defendant's indictment by the inferior court was based on lack of proper scientific foundation by the prosecution in that particular case. In January 1978 this type of evidence was accepted by a court in California (cf. *California* v. *Anderson*, 1978).

The 1977 reversal of the State Supreme Court of Pennsylvania of the case *Pennsylvania* v. *Toppa* (1973) did preclude the use of the method in Pennsylvania until it satisfied the criterion of that court concerning the Frye rule. In that decision, the Pennsylvania Surpeme Court argued that: (a) the human voice is too variable due to effects of physiological, psychological, and environmental changes to produce reliable spectrograms; and (b) the scientific community does not support this method. In the opinion of the author the first argument is a very reasonable one; however, when intratalker variations due to the factors mentioned by the court become so great, a trained examiner will render either a no-opinion decision or, at the worst, a false elimination. A positive identification is therefore not possible under these circumstances. The second argument of the court is controversial and unclarified. Who are the persons forming the "scientific community" concerned with voice identification by spectrography? All those who hold a degree in Audiology and Speech Sciences, or those who practice the method irrespective of their degree? The point of view of the author and other advocates of the system is that the scientific community concerned with a given specialty is formed by those who practice that specialty and not by other people, even by those within the same academic endeavors or professions. Voice identification by subjective methods should be considered an art based on several sciences rather than a branch of a particular science; it is very unlikely that those who do not practice that art or are not very familiar with it can give a well-founded opinion on the matter. No court, certainly, will consider the opinion on problems related to interpretation of a radiograph of the lungs to a physics professor, even if he specializes in electromagnetic radiations (including x-rays).

In this context it should be pointed out that at the present moment there are approximately 18 professional examiners certified to practice the method; in addition, about 20 Ph.D.'s and a comparable number of persons with master's and bachelor's degrees in Audiology and Speech Sciences who are very knowledgeable in voice identification by speech spectrograms support the method provided it is performed properly. It is relevant to quote here Dr. Karl Kryter, the 1973 President of the Acoustical Society of America, who wrote on 23 March of that year to Mr. Henry Greene, Executive Assistant United States Attorney:

> . . . contrary to that resolution [a resolution from several members of the Acoustical Society of America who unofficially expressed the opinion that voiceprints have not yet been proven to be sufficiently valid and reliable for positive speaker identification], it can be stated, in my opinion, that by scientific tests it has been proven within normal standards of statistical reliability and validity, that voiceprints for some speakers, under certain conditions and with certain analysis procedures, can provide positive identification (Tosi et al., J. Acoustical Society of America 51, 2030–2043, 1972). At the same time it should be noted that: (1) as the procedures deviate from those used by the Michigan State University and the Michigan State Police Voiceprint interpreters, the greater the errors and difficulty in making correct voiceprint matches (Hazen, Ph.D. dissertation, State University of New York at Buffalo, 1972); and (2) the imposition of noise or other distortions upon the recorded voice signals and deliberate voice imitations can, but not necessarily, also make decisions about voiceprint matches difficult and subject to some error. On the other hand, and for this latter reason, competent voiceprint interpreters reject as "uncertain" and inadequate for use many voiceprints in order to avoid related errors . . .

On the other hand, a group of speech scientists who are very active and vociferous against voice identification by aural and spec-

trographic examination of speech samples try to recruit other colleagues to their side, very often successfully. The point is that in
order to offer a well-founded opinion on the validity of the method
it is essential to have practical experience in dealing with it. Most
opponents lack this type of expertise or at least a first-hand knowledge. The Supreme Court of Pennsylvania disregarded opinions like
the one by Dr. Kryter and made the reversal in the *Toppa* case.
(This defendant was subsequently tried again, the second time without voice identification evidence and was again fund guilty, although
the jury took considerably more time to reach the verdict as compared with the time taken in the first trial.)

Significantly, a few weeks after the reversal of this case, the
state of Mississippi did accept voice identification evidence by
speech spectrograms in a first impression case (*Mississippi* v. *Widdham*, 1977). In this case the court, aware of the recent Supreme
Court of Pennsylvania reversal, found, nevertheless, that the
method of voice identification by speech spectrograms did satisfy
the Frye rule. In this instance there were three persons suspected
of bomb threat calls to an industrial plant. One of the suspected
persons was held on charges that the criminal phone calls had been
traced to his telephone. This person, as well as another suspected
individual, were eliminated by Lt. Smrkovski after examining their
voices; the third one, Mr. Widdham, was identified as being the
unknown caller. The defense is this trial produced two expert
witnesses, one of them a prominent speech scientist who is absolutely opposed to the method. There was a hung jury in this case.

The Supreme Court of Michigan in 1977 reversed the decision
concerning the case *Michigan* v. *Tobey* (1973). This court based the
reversal, again, on failure of voice identification by speech spectrograms to comply with its particular criterion concerning the Frye
rule, assuming that only two persons were using voice identification
by speech spectrograms and that they were "interested" parties
because their livelihood depended on voice identification, therefore
lacking "impartiality."[4] They ruled that in the future if "disinterested scientists" will express their approval, the method can be
used again in Michigan. A question might arise, however, as to how
a "disinterested scientist" could ever express a valid opinion on a

---

[4] One of the two persons mentioned was a police officer who received his salary
irrespective of his particular function in the crime laboratory and who was forbidden
by law to charge any fee for testifying in a court of law.

subject that does not appeal to his interest. Maybe this is only a matter of semantics, but in any case the Supreme Court of Michigan made several obvious errors in the decision, showing a lack of information on the matter.

The Supreme Court of Massachusetts upheld (1975) the guilty verdict by the appellate court in the case *Commonwealth* v. *Lykus* (1973). Also, the supreme courts of Minnesota and New Jersey upheld the use of "voiceprints" in the *Trimble* case and in the *Andretta* case, respectively. Additionally, there were some decisions reversed and some upheld as well by appellate courts, as listed in Appendix A.

Expert witnesses opposing voice identification by spectrograms are in most cases a definite group of persons; especially a conspicuous couple of them who are very adamantly opposed to the system. One of these two adversary expert witnesses is a prominent speech scientist who constantly organizes the opposition against voice identification by spectrography on the grounds that it lacks any validity, and is actually a "hoax" perpetrated on the people. He was instrumental in the creation of an association, the Academy for Forensic Application of Communication Sciences (AFACS); however, the purposes of that association, according to its bylaws, are of a much larger scope than simply combating voice identification by spectrography; apparently not all of its members (about 55) oppose that method. At the 1977 meeting of the AFACS a debate on "voiceprints" was organized. Dr. Howard Rothman represented the opposition; the author (also a member of the AFACS) spoke in favor of the method. Several persons (including a judge and a law professor) formed the panel; moderator was Mr. Owen Greenspan, an officer from the New York City Police Department. The judge and the law professor expressed their opposition to voice identification by spectrography, but in general the atmosphere of the debate was a constructive one. It is to be hoped that, through the contributions from moderate members of both fractions, the existing gap can be closed. Opposition can contribute greatly to improving this subjective method by providing constructive criticism despite the overall negative emotional response. Also, the presence of adversary expert witnesses in a court of law is desirable for our system of justice. Exposing the jury to the two opposite points of view can eliminate the danger of excessive weight being put on voice identification evidence. However, the author feels that it is of no use for a scientist to simply declare that the system does not work if that scientist cannot back his statements with practice in this specific field, at least comparable with that experienced by professional examiners certified by the IAVI.

In 1974 the Institute of Voice Identification (IVI) was created at Michigan State University (MSU) with the purpose of training persons in this field and producing research in any method of voice identification, including, of course, objective methods. Periodically the MSU-IVI organizes 1-month long workshops to provide training. Workshops are on a full-time basis, 8 hours a day. Workshops are open to any interested person who demonstrates the necessary background to undertake the course. Scientists and crime laboratory technicians from the U.S. and abroad have attended these workshops. Lawyers are also welcomed. (More information is offered in the section on "Training of Voice Identification Examiners" in Chapter 4.)

FUTURE OF VOICE IDENTIFICATION

Nobody expects crime to decrease in the future and criminals of all types will continue to use their voices in the commission of their crimes. Bomb threats, extortions, and hard drug trafficking among the major crimes, and harassment and obscene phone calls among the petty ones, are not possible without voice communication. Therefore, the interest in methods and personnel that can perform efficiently in tasks of voice identification and elimination will increase rather than decrease in the future. Objective methods of voice identification using the ubiquitous computer show promise. Presently, these objective methods are not yet ready to go into the courtroom, but there is no doubt that after being perfected they will be used for producing legal voice identification evidence. However, it is very unlikely that only one type of method of voice identification, whether objective or subjective, will be used exclusively in practical cases. In addition, automatic methods will also require trained examiners. A technician who just inserts the tapes with the "unknown" and known samples into the system, pushes a button, and waits until the computer gives an answer of "same" or "different," as believed possible by some persons, is unrealistic. In 1972 a corporation offered to build such a system for the Law Enforcement Assistance Administration (LEAA), promising that within 1 year it could be implemented. At that time the LEAA requested the opinion of this author on that matter. Such opinion was expressed in a report (Tosi, 1973), indicating that:

> . . . indeed studies on objective methods should be encouraged and funded, but it would be unrealistic to think that in the near future they could be implemented for practical purposes requiring no trained operators . . .

This 1973 opinion can be repeated again in 1978. Furthermore, it can be stated that no method or combination of methods will ever yield a positive result (identification or elimination) in 100% of the cases examined.

Concomitantly, it is reasonable to assume that the number of trained practitioners in voice identification will increase in the future. These practitioners will not be speech scientists but rather highly specialized voice examiners, knowledgeable in speech sciences; they would have to properly prepare the voice samples prior to attempting an examination. This preparation might consist of temporally segmenting, filtering, preemphasizing, eliminating noise and influence of response curve charactertistics of transmitting and recording media when possible, etc. These operations have to be performed by a person; they can hardly be performed automatically by the present or the near-future generation of computers. The human element is still crucial for voice identification and it will be for years to come. After these preparatory operations are completed, the practitioners of the future would decide by *perceptual means* whether or not the samples can be submitted to computer analysis and, if so, what kind of algorithm or combination of algorithms would be the optimal ones in each particular case. Still, the examiner would have the last word for interpretation of computer results. In addition, in the final stage of the voice examination the courtroom witness stand will be occupied by the examiner, not by the computer; the examiner would have to answer the questions from direct and cross-examinations. It is quite obvious then that the practitioner of the future would be closer to the present type of examiner certified by the IAVI than to a computer operator. If this is the case, possibly such an examiner of the future would prefer to use both objective and subjective methods concurrently. Indeed, aural and spectrographic examination can indicate many characteristics of the voice samples in simpler and more direct ways than the computer could. On the other hand, objective methods have better assets than the subjective ones in many other aspects, such as accurate indication of the percentage of error, lack of any kind of bias, and consistency. Therefore, the optimal type of examination of the future might take the best of the two worlds by using concurrently subjective and objective methods and very well trained examiners. These examiners have to be trained, tested, and certified in order that the quality of voice examinations is properly maintained. Up to the present the only institution that has attempted to undertake this mission is the IAVI. It seems that the legal system and the interested parties should consider taking advantage of the years of experience in this matter that this association possesses and to further encourage the reaching of its goal: to provide reliable, unbiased, and well-trained examiners for both prosecution and defense. It is hoped that in the future this alternative will become a reality.

In the meantime, the only system presently utilized in the courtroom—aural and spectrographic examination of speech samples—no doubt will continue to be admitted by courts in the U.S. and abroad because it fulfills a need of the legal system that cannot be ignored on the basis of the belief of some opponents who claim that "it does not work" without having real, first-hand knowledge of the technique. There is no doubt that this subjective method has many shortcomings and that it is only as good and as valid as the examiner is. The arguments that it is unreliable because the human voice is variable and affected by physiological, psychological, resonant, and noisy conditions are unrealistic and based on lack of practical experience, in the opinion of the author. Exactly the same thing could be stated for the objective methods that deserve the unconditional admiration of the opponents to subjective methods. It must be emphasized that as yet the ideal system and efficient parameters for voice identification, invariant and resistant to all these circumstances, have not been found; they will not be found in the predictable future, and possibly they will never be found, because chances are that they simply do not exist.

The rational solution, therefore, to fulfilling the urgent needs of the legal system consists of perfecting the testing ability of the voice identification examiner, plotting his ROC, making sure that only in cases "beyond reasonable doubt" will evidence be presented in a court of law, and ensuring by means of a balanced presentation that the jury not be unduly impressed by this type of evidence, i.e., making sure they are aware that a possibility of error always exists, whatever method or combination of methods (subjective or objective) are used to identify or eliminate a known voice as being the same as the unknown one.

The author believes that the moderate individuals from both sides, opponents and advocates of subjective methods, will make joint efforts to perfect all systems of voice identification to "protect the innocent and to indict the criminal."

Appendix A

COURT CASES INVOLVING VOICE IDENTIFICATION EVIDENCE

From 1966 to December 1970

State v. *Rispoli and Straehle,* State of New York, Westchester County Court; White Plains, NY, 1966
Expert witness for the prosecution: Mr. Lawrence Kersta

U.S. Securities and Exchange Commission v. *Klopp*; Cleveland, OH, 1966
Expert witness for the defense: Mr. Lawrence Kersta
Expert witness appointed by the court: Dr. Oscar Tosi

U.S. v. *Wright,* case 17 U.S. CMA 183,37 C.M.R. 447; CA, 1967
Expert witness for the prosecution: Mr. Lawrence Kersta

State v. *Cary,* case 239 A. 2d 680,685; Elizabeth, NJ, 1968
Expert witness for the prosecution: Mr. Lawrence Kersta
Expert witness appointed by the court: Dr. Oscar Tosi

People v. *King,* case 13588, App. 2nd Div. 2; Los Angeles, CA, 1968
Expert witness for the prosecution: Mr. Lawrence Kersta
Expert witness for the defense: Dr. Peter Ladefoged

State v. *Krapp,* Somerset County Court; Somerville, NJ, 1969
Expert witness for the prosecution: Mr. Lawrence Kersta

State v. *Yarmark,* Essex County Court; Newark, NJ, 1969
Expert witness for the prosecution: Mr. Lawrence Kersta

State v. *DiGiglio,* Middlesex County Court; New Brunswick, NJ, 1970
Expert witness for the defense: Dr. Oscar Tosi
Expert witness for the prosecution: Mr. Lawrence Kersta

From December 1970 to February 1978

Minnesota v. *Constance Trimble,* Ramsey Co. Dist. Ct., St. Paul, No. 24,049
Charge: Murder
Judge: Hon. Harold Schultz, 2nd. Dist., Ramsey Co.
Expert witnesses: D/Lt. Ernest W. Nash and Dr. Oscar Tosi for the prosecution; Dr. Peter Ladefoged for the defense
Hearing: 12 December 1970
Affirmed: Minn. Sup. Ct., No. 265-1/2, filed 26 November 1971
Trial: 28 January 1971
Verdict: Guilty of telephone call, but not guilty of murder charge, 16 March 1972

U.S. v. *Betty Phoenix,* So. Dist. Indiana, No. 70-Cr-428
Charge: Bomb threats
Judge: Hon. A. Dillin, U.S. District Judge
Expert witnesses: D/Lt. Ernest W. Nash and Dr. Oscar Tosi for the prosecution
Verdict: Guilty by jury, 15 April 1971

Florida v. *Joseph Worley,* Orange Co. Ct. of Crim. Juris., No. 70-1095
Charge: Bomb threats
Judge: Hon. Warren Edwards
Expert witnesses: D/Lt. Ernest W. Nash and Dr. Oscar Tosi for the
prosecution
Verdict: Guilty by jury, 4 May 1971
Affirmed: Dist. Ct. App., 4th Dist., Florida, 16 May 1972, No. 71-527
Florida v. *Jose Alea et al.,* Dade Co. Ct. of Crim. Juris., Miami, No. 70-9397
Charges: Conspiracy to commit extortion, Extortion
Judge: Hon. Jack Turner
Expert witnesses: Dr. Oscar Tosi and D/Lt. Ernest W. Nash for the
prosecution
Verdict: Guilty by judge, 18 September 1971
Affirmed: Dist. Ct. App., 3rd Dist., 25 July 1972
Illinois v. *Richard Merholz,* Cir. Ct., 2nd Dist., Cook Co., Evanston, Nos.
72-MC2-52660 and 52661
Charge: Robbery
Judge: Hon. John Limperis
Expert witness: D/Lt. Ernest W. Nash for the prosecution
Hearing: 9 August 1971; Held sound spectrograms testimony admissable
in court for preliminary examination
U.S. v. *Albert Raymond and Roland Addison,* U.S. Dist. Ct. of Columbia,
Washington, DC, No. 800-71
Charge: Attempted murder of a police officer
Expert witnesses: D/Lt. Ernest W. Nash and Dr. Oscar Tosi for the
prosecution; Dr. Gordon Stewart for the defense
Trial: 15 December 1971
Verdict: Guilty by jury, 23 December 1971
Appealed: To U.S. District Ct. App., Washington, D.C., No. 72-1678
Affirmed: Conviction upheld; voice identification by speech spectro-
grams evidence ruled as inadmissible; decided 6 June 1974
New Jersey v. *Armond Faugno and Thomas Andretta,* Middlesex Co. Ct.,
New Brunswick Cr. Nos. I 445-66 and I 446-66
Charges: Extortion, Threatening to take a life
Judge: Hon. John B. Molineux, JCC
Expert witnesses: D/Lt. Ernest W. Nash, Dr. Oscar Tosi, and Dr. Peter
Ladefoged for the prosecution
Trial: Dr. Tosi and D/Lt. Nash qualified as experts and their testimony
admitted reference the reliability of voice identification by speech
spectrograms; Judge Molineux denied prosecution's request for order
requiring defendants to make voice recordings for voiceprint analyses
Appealed: Sup. Ct., Dr. Flannagan and Dr. Denes for the defense
Affirmed: Sup. Ct. A-40, 1973, filed 13 November 1972, reported as *New
Jersey* v. *Andretta and Faugno;* this decision reversed Judge Molineux
and ordered voice recordings and reversed an earlier stand in *New
Jersey* v. *Cary*
Case was suspended because one defendant committed suicide and the
other disappeared.

Louisiana v. *Rallie C. Edwins,* Dist. Ct., E. Baton Rouge Parish, Baton Rouge
  Charge: Bribery (offer to destroy tax record in the Department of Internal Revenue files amounting to $1,104,000)
  Judge: Hon. Donovan Parker
  Expert witnesses: D/Lt. Ernest W. Nash for the prosecution; Dr. Gunn for the defense
  Hearing: 6 January 1972; case was dismissed
Missouri v. *Fred Lee Crowe,* Cir. Ct., Co. of St. Louis, No. 315868
  Charge: Extortion (telephone calls demanding $40,000 or one son would be killed)
  Judge: Hon. John J. Kelley, Jr.
  Prosecutor: Assistant Noel Robyn
  Defense Attorney: Sam VanDover
  Expert witnesses: Dr. Oscar Tosi and D/Lt. Ernest W. Nash for the prosecution
California v. *Jack D. Coffey,* Mun. Ct., Alameda Co., Fremont
  Charge: Obscene telephone calls
  Judge: John Weber (Ruled voiceprints admissible and D/Lt. Nash a qualified expert in the use of voiceprints)
  Prosecutor: Assistant Michael Semansky
  Defense Attorney: Roy Hamrick
  Expert witnesses: Dr. Peter Ladefoged and D/Lt. Ernest W. Nash for the prosecution; Dr. Michael Hecker, amicus curiae
  Hearing: 23 February 1972; defendant pleaded guilty
Wisconsin v. *Brian Hussong,* Cir. Ct., Br. No. 2, Brown Co., Green Bay
  Charge: Murder
  Judge: Hon. Robert Parins
  Prosecutor: Donald Zuidmueller
  Defense Attorney: Mr. Pressintein
  Expert witness: D/Lt. Ernest W. Nash for the prosecution
  Verdict: Guilty by jury, 13 April 1972
California v. *Edward D. Law,* Sup. Ct., Dept. No. 1, Fresno Co., Fresno, No. 26331
  Charge: Bomb threat
  Judge: Hon. Blaine Pettit
  Prosecutor: W. Kent Levis
  Defense Attorney: Keith Raymond
  Expert witnesses: Dr. Oscar Tosi, Dr. Peter Ladefoged, and D/Lt. Ernest W. Nash for the prosecution
  Verdict: Guilty by jury, 17 May 1972
  Appealed: The case was appealed to the Fifth Appellate District, California Court of Appeals. On 25 June 1974 the court upheld counts 3 and 4 based on non-voice identification evidence. The case involved a disguised voice; the court reasoned reliability of voice identification evidence involving disguised voices had not yet been determined
Michigan v. *Clifton Patton,* Dist. Ct., 41st Dist., Mt. Clemens, Macomb Co.
  Charge: Threatening calls

Judge: Hon. Adam Nowicki
Prosecutor: Assistant Donald Roberge
Defense Attorney: Thomas Purdo
Expert witnesses: Dr. Oscar Tosi and D/Lt. Ernest W. Nash for the
    prosecution
Verdict: Guilty by judge
Michigan v. *Jerry Delong*, Dist. Ct., 59th Dist., Muskegon Co., Muskegon,
    No. S-2182
Charge: Bomb threat
Judge: Hon. Ralph Rose
Prosecutor: Assistant Gerald Warner
Defense Attorney: Edward Welch
Expert witnesses: Dr. Oscar Tosi and D/Lt. Ernest W. Nash for the
    prosecution
Verdict: Not guilty by jury, 13 June 1972
Michigan v. *Douglas Arthey*, Dist. Ct., 14th Dist., Ann Arbor
Charge: Bomb threat
Judge: Hon. Edward Deake
Prosecutor: Assistant Lynwood Noah
Defense Attorney: Kenneth Morris
Expert witnesses: Dr. Oscar Tosi and D/Lt. Ernest W. Nash for the
    prosecution; Ms. Linda Chiari for the defense
Verdict: Guilty by judge, 14 June 1974
Affirmed: By Circuit Court, 1973
California v. *Charles Watson*, Sup. Ct. No. 5, Sacramento Co.
Charges: Pimping, Pandering, Extortion, Conspiracy to commit extortion
Judge: Hon. Lloyd Phillips
District Attorney: Assistant Bartley Bleuel
Defense Attorney: Charles D'Arcy (public defender)
Expert witness: D/Lt. Ernest W. Nash for the prosecution
Trial: Voice identification evidence presented on 16 June 1972
Verdict: Guilty of pimping, pandering, attempted extortion by jury, 22
    June 1972
Affirmed: By Third District Court of Appeals
Michigan v. *Michael Roberson*, Rec. Ct., Detroit
Charge: Bomb threat
Judge: Hon. John A. Aloisi
Prosecutor: Assistant William Joyce
Defense Attorney: Ronald Gold
Expert witness: D/Lt. Ernest W. Nash for the prosecution
Verdict: Guilty by judge, 12 June 1972
Michigan v. *Frederick Lemon*, 61st. Dist. Ct., Grand Rapids
Charge: False fire alarm
Judge: Hon. Woodrow Yared
Prosecutor: David Kamm (chief trial attorney)
Defense Attorney: Robert Quinn
Expert witnesses: Dr. Oscar Tosi and D/Lt. Ernest W. Nash for the
    prosecution
Verdict: Not guilty by jury, 2 August 1972

California v. *Dewey C. Hodo,* Mun. Ct., 23rd. Div., Riverside Co., No.
10222
   Charge: Misconduct of juror
   Judge: Hon. Roland Wilson
   Prosecutor: Terrance Boren (chief trial attorney)
   Defense Attorney: Arthur Lester
   Expert witnesses: Dr. Oscar Tosi and D/Lt. Ernest W. Nash for the
      prosecution
   Hearing: 3 August 1972, to determine probable cause; Judge Wilson
      found probable cause
   Verdict: Found guilty by judge
South Carolina v. *Lawrence Vice,* Cir. Ct., 9th Dist., Charleston
   Charge: Murder
   Judge: Hon. Nicholson
   County Solicitor: Robert Wallace
   Defense Attorney: Leonard Long
   Expert witness: D/Lt. Ernest W. Nash for the prosecution
   Verdict: Defendant changed plea to Voluntary manslaughter; defense
      counselor admitted into record that his client made the call
Michigan v. *T. C. Smith,* Pro. Ct., Genesee Co., Flint
   Charge: Extortion
   Judge: Hon. Luke Quinn
   Prosecutor: Assistant Seigrist
   Defense Attorney: Michael Kachnykewych
   Expert witness: D/Lt. Ernest W. Nash for the prosecution
   Verdict: Guilty by judge, 28 September 1972
California v. *Steven Chapter,* Cr. 65050, Mun. Ct., Marin Co., San Rafael
   Charge: Bomb threat
   Judge: Hon. Gary Thomas
   District Attorney: Assistant Vernon Smith
   Defense Attorney: Robert Moran
   Expert witnesses: Dr. Oscar Tosi and D/Lt. Ernest W. Nash for the
      prosecution; Dr. Peter Ladefoged, Dr. Michael Hecker, Mr. Fausto
      Poza, Dr. Frank Clarke, Dr. Harry Hollien, and Dr. McGlone for the
      defense
   Hearing: 24 October 1972; judge held the defendant for trial
   Verdict: Superior Judge found Chapter not guilty, disqualifying voice
      identification evidence and pointing out errors in the examination by
      Nash
Crown v. *Vince Montani,* Prov. Ct., Wentworth Co., Hamilton, Ontario,
Canada
   Charge: Extortion
   Judge: Hon. Albert Marck
   Crown Attorney: Anton Zuraw
   Defense Council: John Bowlby
   Expert witness: D/Lt. Ernest W. Nash for the prosecution
   Hearing: 26 October 1972, judge ruled voiceprint evidence acceptable
      and D/Lt. Nash an expert

Trial: 4 February 1974; defendant admitted the identity of his voice on all tapes in question

Note: The defendant (through his attorney) admitted the voice was his. In this case, Drs. Gerstman, Hollien, and McGlone were prepared to testify for the defense. Gerstman and Hollien had been on television and radio explaining their involvement and future testimony. This represents a case of first impression in Canada

California v. *Nehemiah Jackson III, et al.,* Sup. Ct., Riverside Co., Nos. Cr. 9138 & 9485, Indio

Charge: Murder

Judge: Hon. Slaughter

Prosecutor: Terrence Boren (chief trial attorney)

Defense Attorneys: Kenneth Thomas, David Epstein, and Henry Nelson

Expert witnesses: Dr. Oscar Tosi, Dr. John Black, and D/Lt. Ernest W. Nash for the prosecution; Dr. Peter Ladefoged, Dr. Harry Hollien, Dr. Louis Gerstman, Dr. Ralph Vanderslice, Dr. George Papçun, and possibly others for the defense

Verdict: Ended in mistrial—hung jury

Florida v. *Joseph Perkins,* Ct. of Crim. Juris., Dade Co., Miami, No. 72-7333

Charge: Extortion

Judge: Hon. Arthur Huttoe

State's Attorney: Ira Dubitsky

Defense Attorney: Michael Masin

Expert witnesses: Dr. Oscar Tosi and D/Lt. Ernest W. Nash for the prosecution

Trial: Dr. Tosi and D/Lt. Nash testified; evidence and testimony accepted on 17 January 1972

Verdict: Not guilty by jury, 18 January 1973

U.S. v. *Alphonse Sisco et al.,* Dist. Ct., So. Dist. of New York

Charge: Conspiracy to violate narcotic laws

Judge: Hon. Frederick VanPelt Bryan

U.S. Attorney: Mr. McDowal

Defense Attorney: Gino Gallina

Expert witnesses: Dr. Oscar Tosi, Dr. Louis Gerstman, Ms. Linda Chiari, and D/Lt. Ernest W. Nash for the defense; Dr. Barry Hazen and Dr. Ralph Vanderslice called by the United States Government (U.S. judge refused to allow Dr. Hazen to testify)

Trial: 14 February 1973

Verdict: Not guilty of using telephone to further a conspiracy, but guilty of other charges

Arizona v. *Datlo and Dawson,* Superior Ct., Pima Co., Tucson, No. A-22478

Charge: Conspiracy to defraud

Judge: Hon. Richard Roylston

Deputy County Attorney: Richard Michela

Defense Attorney: Howard Kashman

Expert witness: D/Lt. Ernest W. Nash for the prosecution

Hearing: 14 March 1973, judge held defendants for trial and ruled voice
identification admissible. Also, defendants were granted separate trials
Verdict: Jury found Datlo guilty on 17 April 1973; Dawson pending
Michigan v. *Frederick A. Kramer,* 16th Dist. Ct., Co. of Wayne, City of
Livonia, No. 492-730019
Charge: Extortion
Judge: Hon. James Mies
Prosecutor: Assistant Varskin Baydarian
Defense Attorney: Marvin Blake
Expert witness: D/Lt. Ernest W. Nash for the prosecution
Hearing: 16 March 1973; Kramer changed plea to guilty
U.S. v. *Max Britton et al.,* Dist. Ct., Western Dist. of Tennessee, Memphis,
No. Cr. 72-48
Charge: Bombings
Judge: Hon. Bailey Brown
U.S. Attorney: Assistant Larry E. Parrish
Defense Attorneys: Al Hargey, Robert Andrews, and Howard Paul
Expert witness: D/Lt. Ernest W. Nash for the prosecution
Trial: 19 March 1973
Verdict: Jury found defendants guilty on three counts of conspiracy to
bomb
Affirmed: 12 February 1975, Sixth Federal Circuit Court of Appeals
Commonwealth v. *Francis Vitello et al.,* Superior Ct., Suffolk Co., Boston,
Massachusetts
Charge: Conspiracy to violate gambling laws
Judge: Hon. James Roy
District Attorneys: Jack Gaffney and Tom Dwyer
Defense Attorneys: led by Mr. Demento
Expert witnesses: Dr. Oscar Tosi and D/Lt. Ernest W. Nash for the
prosecution
Hearings: 22 March 1973 and 23 March 1973
Trial: 13 April 1973
Verdict: 19 April 1973; all defendants found guilty
U.S. v. *Timothy Bogner,* Dist. Ct., No. Dist. of Ohio, Toledo, No. CR 73-
10
Charge: Bomb threats
Judge: Hon. Don Young
U.S. Attorney: Assistant Erie D. Chapman III
Defense Attorney: George Royer
Expert witnesses: D/Lt. Ernest W. Nash and D/Sgt. Lonnie Smrkovski
for the prosecution (qualified as experts and their testimony admitted);
Dr. Ivan Harvey for the defense
Verdict: Not guilty by jury, 30 March 1973
Wisconsin v. *Larry Amidon,* County Ct., Br. II, Rock Co., Janesville
Charge: Armed robbery
Judge: Hon. John H. Boyle
Prosecutor: John Sheehan
Defense Attorney: Richard Hemming

Expert witness: D/Lt. Ernest W. Nash for the prosecution
Hearing: 11 April 1973; voice identification evidence admitted
U.S. v. *Clyde Jenkins et al.,* Dist. Ct., Western Dist. of Tennessee, Memphis, Cr-72-45
  Charge: Conspiracy to possess narcotics
  Judge: Hon. Robert McCrie
  U.S. Attorney: Larry Parrish
  Defense Attorney: Larry Friedman
  Expert witness: D/Lt. Ernest W. Nash for the prosecution
  Trial: 14 May 1973
  Verdict: Jury found Jenkins guilty of conspiracy to possess narcotics
Commonwealth of Pennsylvania v. *Adam Andrew Toppa,* Common Pleas
  Ct. for Lackawanna Co., Scranton
  Charge: Murder
  Judge: Hon. Richard Conaboy
  Assistant District Attorneys: Ernest Gazda and William Garvey
  Defense Attorneys: James O'Brien and Peter Loftus
  Expert witness: D/Lt. Ernest W. Nash for the prosecution
  Trial: 6 June 1973
  Verdict: Guilty of murder, first degree
  Appealed: Sup. Ct. of Pennsylvania disqualified voice identification and ordered retrial, in 1977
  Affirmed: Defendant was found guilty in retrial with no voice identification evidence
U.S. v. *Eddie Jackson et al.,* Dist. Ct., Eastern District of Detroit
  Charge: Conspiracy to possess narcotics
  Judges: Hon. Pratt and Feikkens
  U.S. Attorney: Atlee Wampler III
  Defense Attorneys: Rothblatt, Henry, and Halprin
  Expert witnesses: Dr. Oscar Tosi and D/Lt. Ernest W. Nash for the prosecution
  Trial: 21 June 1973; voice identification evidence admitted
  Verdict: Some defendants found guilty
Michigan v. *Bryant,* Rec. Ct., City of Detroit
  Charge: Extortion
  Judge: Hon. Samuel Gardner
  Assistant Prosecutor: Tom Behan
  Defense Attorneys: Pitts and Raines
  Expert witness: D/Lt. Ernest W. Nash for the prosecution
  Hearing: 21 June 1973; defendants bound over for trial
Michigan v. *Plamondon,* Cir. Ct., Wexford County, City of Cadillac
  Charge: Extortion
  Judge: Hon. William Peterson
  Special Prosecuting Attorney: John Wilson
  Defense Attorneys: Ted Hughes and Davis
  Expert witnesses: Dr. Oscar Tosi and D/Lt. Ernest W. Nash for the prosecution
  Hearing: 16 July 1973; testimony was video taped during pretrial hearing to be played to jury after court ruled on admissibility. Judge Peterson ruled acceptance of the process and the identification in this case

Trial: Waived, 18 July 1973
Verdict: Found guilty of extortion, 27 July 1973
Appealed: September 1975; reversed and remanded for new trial; State
  of Michigan Ct. of App., Division III No. 19267-19268
Michigan v. *Tobey,* Cir. Ct. of Washtenaw Co., Ann Arbor
  Charge: Sale of heroin
  Judge: Hon. Ross W. Campbell
  Prosecutor: Lynwood Noah
  Defense Attorney: Norman VanEpps
  Expert witnesses: D/Lt. Ernest W. Nash, D/Sgt. Lonnie Smrkovski, and
    Dr. Oscar Tosi for the prosecution
  Trial:25, 26, 27 July 1973
  Verdict: Guilty by jury, 8 August 1973
  Appealed: Decision reversed by Supreme Court of Michigan in 1977
U.S. v. *Joel J. Clore,* U.S. Dist. Ct., Montgomery, Alabama
  Charge: Bomb threat
  Judge: Hon. Robert Verner
  U.S. Attorney: David Byrne
  Defense Attorney: Mr. Linne
  Expert witnesses: Dr. Oscar Tosi and D/Lt. Ernest W. Nash (qualified
    as experts and testimony admitted reference reliability of voice iden-
    tification); Dr. Louis Gerstman and Dr. Harry Hollien experts for the
    defense, by affidavit
  Trial: 12 November 1973
  Verdict: Not guilty, 15 November 1973

U.S. v. *Garrison et al.,* Southern District Louisiana, New Orleans
  Charge: Bribery
  Jugde: Hon. Herbert Christenberry
  U.S. Attorneys: Gerald Gallinghouse, Michael Ellis, Eric Giselson
  Defense Attorneys: Dr. Fred Barnett, Louis Merhinge, Mr. LaCour
  Expert witnesses: D/Lt. Ernest W. Nash for the prosecution; Dr. Louis
    Gerstman for the defense
  Trial: 23, 24 August 1974

Michigan v. *Chaisson,* Dist. 54-1; City of Lansing
  Charge: Larceny by trick
  Judge: Hon. Charles Felice
  Prosecuting Attorney: Thomas Kulick (Assistant prosecutor)
  Defense Attorney: Thomas Bissell
  Expert witnesses: Dr. Oscar Tosi and D/Lt. Ernest W. Nash for the
    prosecution; Dr. Ehrlick for the defense
  Hearing: 14, 15 July 1973 and 4 September 1973. At suppression hearing,
    defense presented Dr. Harry Hollien, Dr. Stevens, Dr. Louis Gerst-
    man, Dr. Oscar Tosi, and Mr. Fausto Poza. The question of admissi-
    bility was never answered—charge was dismissed by the prosecutor
Michigan v. *LaPuma and Morelli,* Cir. Ct., Oakland Co., Pontiac
  Charges: Extortion, Conspiracy to violate gambling laws
  Judge: Hon. William Beasley
  Prosecuting Attorney: Eugene Friedman
  Defense Attorney: Jack Bain

Expert witnesses: Dr. Oscar Tosi and D/Lt. Ernest W. Nash for the
prosecution (voice identification evidence admitted, but not used in
the trial)

Hearing: 6, 7 September 1973

Commonwealth v. *Edward Lykus,* Sup. Ct., New Bedford, Massachusetts

Charges: Kidnapping, Extortion, Murder

Judge: Hon. James McGuire

District Attorney: Phillip Rollins

Defense Attorney: Ronald Harper

Expert witnesses: Dr. Oscar Tosi and D/Lt. Ernest W. Nash for the
prosecution; Dr. Louis Gerstman for the defense

Trial: 22 September 1973

Verdict: 18 October 1973. Defendant found guilty of first degree murder,
kidnapping, and extortion

Affirmed: By the Massachusetts Supreme Court on 27 March 1975;
Opinion written by Justice Hennessy

U.S. v. *Vincent Doss,* Western Dist. of Tennessee, Memphis

Charges: Counterfeiting, Bribing a federal witness

Judge: Hon. Robert McCrea

U.S. Attorneys: Larry Parrish and H. Ewing

Defense Attorneys: Robert Andrews and S. Catanzaro

Expert witness: D/Lt. Ernest W. Nash for the prosecution

Hearing: 23, 25 September 1973

Trial: 15 January 1974

Verdict: Guilty

California v. *Brannon and Kelly,* Sup. Ct., Santa Ana, Orange Co.

Charges: Extortion, Bookmaking

Judge: Everett W. Dickey

Assistant District Attorney: William Evans

Defense Attorneys: Peter Brown, John Downer, Arnold Hewett

Expert witness: D/Lt. Ernest W. Nash for the prosecution

Trial: 17, 18, 23, 24 October 1973

Verdict: Brannon and Kelly pled guilty on 18 December 1973

Appealed: California Court of Appeals, 4th Appellate District

Affirmed: 18 June 1975

U.S. v. *Charles Anderson et al.,* U.S. Dist. Ct., Dist. of Columbia, Washington, DC

Charges: Bribery of public officials, Conspiracy to violate gambling laws

Judge: Hon. John H. Pratt

Assistant U.S. Attorneys: S/A Allan Early III, Ted Wieseman

Defense Attorneys: Edward Williams et al.

Expert witness: D/Lt. Ernest W. Nash for the prosecution

Hearing: 17-18 December 1973

Trial: 2-3 January 1973

Verdict: Some defendants were found guilty

Michigan v. *Richard Parsons,* 53rd. Dist. Ct., Howell

Charge: Making obscene and threatening telephone calls

Judge: Hon. Richardson Robinson

Prosecuting Attorney: Mr. James Burnett

Defense Attorney: Mr. James Barley
Expert witness: D/Sgt. Lonnie Smrkovski for the prosecution
Trial: January 1974 (nonjury trial)
Verdict: Found guilty of making obscene and threatening telephone calls, 8 January 1974
Illinois v. *Thomas Knott,* No. 73-CF-37, Cir. Ct., Kendall County, Yorkville
Charge: Murder
Judge: Hon. James Boyle
State's Attorney: Roy Lasswell
Action: Suppression hearing
Expert witness: D/Lt. Ernest W. Nash for the prosecution; Dr. George Papçun for the defense
Trial: 21, 22 March 1974
Verdict: Jury returned verdict of not guilty, 22 March 1974
U.S. v. *Harold James Jordan,* No. 47664, U.S. Dist. Ct., Eastern Dist. So. Div., Detroit, Michigan
Charge: Bomb threat
Judge: Hon. Feikens
U.S. Attorney: Gordon Gold
Defense Attorney: Jim Roberts
Expert witness: Dr. Oscar Tosi and D/Lt. Ernest W. Nash for the prosecution
Hearing: 28 January 1974; voice identification evidence admitted
U.S. v. *Earl F. Brown, Jr.,* U.S. Dist. Ct., Eastern Dist. of Tennessee, No. 13130
Charge: Possession and sale of untaxed whiskey
Judge: Hon. Charles Neese
Assistant U.S. Attorney: Lloyd Stanley
Defense Attorney: Jerry Summers
Expert witness: D/Lt. Ernest W. Nash for the prosecution
Verdict: Ended in hung jury, 31 January 1974
Louisiana v. *Jerome Winberg,* Crim. Dist. Ct. for Parish of New Orleans, Sec. D—New Orleans
Charge: Corruption and misconduct of a public official
Judge: Hon. William G. Swift
Prosecutors: Julian Murray, Glen Burns, Wens Parra
Defense Attorneys: John Martzell, Robert Glass, Mike Hertzog, Jerome Winsberg
Expert witness: D/Sgt. Lonnie Smrkovski for the prosecution
Trial: 4, 5, 6, 7 February 1974
Verdict: Found not guilty by jury on 7 February 1974
U.S. v. *John B. Sample, Jr.,* 71-575, Eastern Dist. of Pennsylvania, City of Philadelphia
Charges: Forgery, Stealing government checks
Judge: Hon. Daniel Huyett III
Assistant U.S. Attorney: Gary Tilles
Defense Attorney: Fred Herman
Expert witness: D/Lt. Ernest W. Nash for the prosecution

Trial: 1 April 1974
Verdict: Guilty
Michigan v. Robert William Carroll, 73-04339, Rec. Ct., Detroit
Charge: Larceny in a building
Judge: Hon. Thomas L. Poindexter
Expert witness: D/Lt. Ernest W. Nash for the prosecution
Verdict: Defendant pled nolo contendere, 3 June 1974
People of the State of Michigan v. William John Chorkey, 52nd Dist. Ct.,
Walled Lake
Charge: Bomb threats
Judge: Hon. Martin L. Boyle
Expert witness: D/Sgt. Malcolm E. Hall for the prosecution
Trial: 12-13 August 1975
Verdict: Not guilty
Note: Expert testimony held as prejudicial to the defense because, pros-
ecution failed to declare use of expert testimony; therefore, evidence
not admissible
Michigan v. Larry Nelson, Cir. Ct., Co. of Oakland
Charge: Extortion
Judge: Hon. Frederick C. Ziem
Prosecutor: Keith Corbett
Defense Attorney: Howard Arnkoff
Expert witnesses: Dr. Oscar Tosi, D/Sgt. Lonnie Smrkovski, and Dr.
Len Jansen for the prosecution
Trial: 18-19 August 1975
Verdict: Guilty, 25 August 1975
Crown v. David Medvidew, Court of Queen's Bench, Brandon, Manitoba,
Canada
Charges: Bomb threat, Conveying a false message
Judge: Justice Jimmie Wilson
Crown Attorneys: Mr. Lawrence McInnes and Mr. Jerry Bowring
Defense Attorney: Mr. Robert Haynes
Expert witnesses: D/Sgt. Lonnie Smrkovski and Dr. Henry Truby for
the Crown; Dr. Harry Hollien for the defense (qualified as an expert
in human speech sound production)
Trial: 22-26 March 1976
Jury Verdict: Guilty
Connecticut v. Charles R. Calver, Ct. of Common Pleas, G.A. 10 CR82414,
Norwich
Charge: False fire reports (2 counts)
Judge: Hon. Lenny Dorsey
Prosecutor: Austin J. McGuigan
Defense: Public defender
Expert witness: D/Lt. Lonnie Smrkovski for the prosecution
Trial: Set for 4 June 1976
Verdict: On 3 June 1976, a plea of guilty was entered by Calver to both
counts
U.S. v. Nolan Ray Williamson, U.S. Dist. Ct., Western Dist. of Tennessee,
Memphis CR72-45

Charge: Conspiracy to violate narcotics laws
U.S. Attorney: Larry Parrish
Defense Attorney: Joe Dycus
Expert witnesses: D/Sgt. Malcolm E. Hall and D/Lt. Ernest W. Nash for
  the prosecution
Trial: August 1975
Verdict: Found guilty, sentenced to ten years

U.S. v. *Lucas,* Federal Court, Southern District, New York
Charge: Conspiracy to violate narcotics law
Defense Attorney: J. Hoffman
Expert witnesses: Dr. Oscar Tosi for the defense; Dr. Weiss for the
  prosecution
Verdict: Not guilty
Note: In this case expert witness for the defense was able to demonstrate
  tampering with evidence tape recorded by an informer

Maryland v. *James Reed, Jr.,* Montgomery Co. Cir. Ct., Rockville
Charges: Rape, Extortion
Judge: Hon. John McAuliffee
State's Attorney: Steve Shaw
Defense Attorney: William Wood
Expert witnesses (hearing): D/Lt. Lonnie Smrkovski, Dr. John McClung,
  and Dr. Oscar Tosi for the state; Dr. Donald Baker for the defense
Hearing: 28, 29 July 1975; On 9 September 1975 Judge McAuliffe ruled
  the evidence admissible
Expert witnesses (trial): D/Lt. Lonnie Smrkovski and Dr. Oscar Tosi for
  the state
Other witnesses (trial): Dr. Donald Baker and Mr. Fausto Poza (the court
  would not allow either to testify as experts in voice identification)
Trial: 27 October-3 November 1975
Verdict Hung jury
Plea: Guilty by reason of insanity, 28 December 1975

U.S. v. *Carlos Valle,* Southern District of New York 1975
Expert witness: Mr. Fred Lundgren for the prosecution
Verdict: Hung jury; in a retrial defendant was found guilty

Colorado v. *L. Cunningham* (29 April 1976)
Expert witness: Mr. Fred Lundgren for the prosecution
Verdict: Guilty

Connecticut v. *Gold,* Waterbury
Charge: Murder
Prosecutor: F. McDonald
Defense Attorney: William Kunstler
Expert witness: Dr. Oscar Tosi for the prosecution
Trial: November 1976
Verdict: Found guilty of murder by jury

Oregon v. *V. Hanna,* Portland, C77-503-248-3162
Charge: Extortion
Judge: Hon. J. Ellis

Prosecutor: Bruce L. Byerly
Defense Attorney: J. Duncan
Expert witnesses: Dr. Oscar Tosi and Mr. Fred Lundgren for the prosecution; Dr. Leland C. and Jensen for the defense
Trial: November 1976
Verdict: Guilty

Maine v. *T. V. Williams,* Augusta
Judge: Hon. Lewis Naiman
Prosecutor: Joseph M. Jalar
Defense Attorneys: Emmet O'Gara and James Harrington
Expert witnesses: Dr. Oscar Tosi and D/Lt. Lonnie Smrkovski for the prosecution; Dr. Louis Gerstman, Mr. Fausto Poza for the defense
Trial: December 1976
Verdict: Found guilty of terrorizing, by jury
Affirmed: Sup. Ct. of Maine

Air Force v. *S. Garneo,* Air Force Base of Nebraska, Military Court (1976)
Charge: Bomb threat
Expert witness: Mr. Fred Lundgren for the prosecution
Verdict: Not guilty

Florida v. *Otero,* Dade County, Miami
Charge: Bombing
Judge: Hon. C. Wells (Walton Beach, Okaloosa Co., Fl.)
Prosecutor: G. Yoss
Defense Attorneys: Public Defenders W. Clay, R. Rosenblatt, and L. Cooperman
Expert witnesses: D/Lt. Lonnie Smrkovski for the prosecution; Dr. Oscar Tosi for the defense
Trial: 9 January 1977
Verdict: Defendant acquitted from the criminal call
Note: Both the expert witness for the defense and for the prosecution arrived independently at the conclusion that the "unknown" criminal voice was different from the voice of the defendant

U.S. v. *McKinely,* 10th Federal Cir. Ct., Oklahoma City, Oklahoma
Charge: Extortion
Judge: Hon. P. Daugherty
Prosecutor: Susie Pritchett
Defense Attorney: R. Burger
Expert witesses: Dr. Oscar Tosi and Mr. Fred Lundgren for the prosecution
Trial: 10 February 1977
Verdict: Guilty

Mississippi v. *Widdham,* Co. of Atala, Kosciusko
Charge: Bomb threats
Judge: Hon. C. Morgan
District Attorney: N. McNeil
Defense Attorney: W. Brook
Expert witnesses: Dr. Oscar Tosi and D/Lt. Lonnie Smrkovski for the prosecution; Dr. Harry Hollien for the defense

Trial: March 1977
Verdict: Hung jury
Note: In this case two suspected persons, one of them in prison, were eliminated by the prosecution expert witnesses

Virginia v. *Saunders,* Hanover Co., Ashland
Charge: Making obscene telephone calls
Judge: Hon. J. Landram
Prosecutor: G. Johnson
Defense Attorney: D. Dohnae
Expert witnesses: Dr. Oscar Tosi and Mr. Fred Lundgren for the prosecution
Trial: April 1977
Verdict: Guilty

U.S. v. *Isaiah Williams and Michael Manning,* Southern Dist. of New York
Charge: Narcotics
Judge: Hon. J. Broderick
Prosecutor: David Paterson
Defense Attorney: S. Rosenbaum
Expert witnesses: Dr. Oscar Tosi, Dr. Henry Truby, and Mr. Fred Lundgren for the prosecution; Dr. Louis Gerstman for the defense
Trial: December 1977
Verdict: Guilty

U.S. v. *Leroy Barnes et al.,* South District of New York, U.S. Federal Court, S-77, CR 190 (HFW)
Charge:
Judge: Hon. Henry Werker
Prosecutors: Robert Fisk, Robert Mazur
Defense Attorneys: David Breitbaitet and associates
Expert witness: Dr. L. Gerstman for the defense
Consultant for the government: D/Lt. Lonnie Smrkvoski
Trial: 19 September—November 1977
Verdict: Guilty
Note: Dr. Gerstman stated that the unknown voice was not the same as the defendant's voice, based on his short-term memory aural examination. He stated under oath he has produced the same type of evidence about 5 times

California v. *Harold Anderson,* case No. 6071, Mun. Ct., Sacramento
Charge: False Report of emergency
Judge: Hon. Raul Ramirez
Prosecutor: Kit Cleand
Defense Attorney: D. Simmons
Expert witnesses: Mr. Fausto Poza and Dr. George Papçun for the prosecution; Dr. Henry Truby and Ms. Linda Chiari for the defense
Verdict: Guilty
Note: The Court stated that requirements for admission of voice identification by speech spectrograms, as demanded by the Supreme Court of California in the Kelly case, had been fulfilled in this case. Poza and Papçun identified the voice of the defendant as being the same as the unknown voice

Ohio v. *Henry Trussell,* Montgomery Co., Common Pleas Ct., Dayton, Court No. 3118
Judge: Hon. John Meagher
Prosecutors: James Brogan and Dennis Langer
Defense Attorney: Jack Patricoff
Expert witnesses: D/Lt. Lonnie Smrkovski and Dr. Harry Hollien for the defense
Trial: 16, 17 February 1978
Verdict: Guilty, sentenced to 1-10 years
Ohio v. *Thomas Wilkinson et al.,* Common Pleas Ct., Portsmouth, Case No. CR 77-79
Charge: Violation of narcotics laws
Judge: Hon. William Ammer
Prosecutor: Lynn Grimshaw
Defense Attorneys: Roger Clark and Lawrence Kimble
Expert witnesses: Dr. Oscar Tosi and D/Lt. Lonnie Smrkovski for the prosecution; Dr. John W. Perkins for the defense
Trial: 23-29 February 1978
Verdict: Guilty

APPELLATE COURT DECISIONS ON VOICE IDENTIFICATION EVIDENCE FROM 1970 TO PRESENT

State

Worley v. *State of California,* Fourth District Court of Appeals, No. 71527, decided 19 May 1972 (263 S. 2d 613); upheld
Alea v. *State,* District Court of Appeals of Florida, Third District, No. 71-1419, decided 25 July 1972 (265 S. 2nd 96); upheld
Dewy Hodo v. *Superior Court,* Court of Appeals, Fourth District, Second Division, State of California, No. 4 Civil 12397, decided 22 February 1973; upheld
Charles William Watson v. *State,* Court of Appeals of California, Third Appellate District, Sacramento, Criminal No. 3 6688, Supreme Court No. 40787, May 1973; upheld
E. D. Law v. *People* Court of Appeals of the State of California, Fifth Appellate District, No. 5. Criminal 1516, decided 25 June 1974; reversed due to mimicking

Federal

Moses Brown, Jr. v. *United States,* Superior Court of the District of Columbia, Criminal No. 34383-72, decided 1 May 1973; upheld

Addison and Raymond v. *United States,* U.S. Court of Appeals for the District of Columbia Circuit, Nos. 72-1579 and 72-1678, decided 6 June 1974; reversed

M. Britton et al., v. *United States,* 6th Federal Circuit Court of Appeals, February 1975; conviction confirmed

C. Baller v. *United States,* 4th Federal Circuit Court of Appeals, 1975; conviction confirmed

Appendix B

Following is a list, as of 1977, of members and trainees of the IAVI who might conduct voice identification examination by aural and spectrographic examination of speech samples for either the prosecution or the defense, and/or present evidence in court if qualified by the IAVI.

In the USA:

Dr. Peter Ladefoged (University of California, Los Angeles)
Dr. George Papçun (University of California, Los Angeles)
Mr. Jack Percy (Los Angeles Police Department, California)
Mr. David Paige (Connecticut State Police, Connecticut)
Dr. Henry Truby (Florida University, Miami, Florida)
Mr. Roger Parian (Georgia State Crime Laboratory, Savannah, Georgia)
Dr. William Lashbrook (University of Illinois, Normal)
Dr. Michael Hosiko (Department of Speech Pathology and Audiology, University of Illinois, Carbondale)
Mr. Marlon Miller (Elkhart Co. Sheriff Department, Goshen, Indiana)
Mr. William Klein (Kentucky State Police, Kentucky)
Mr. Lelend Denison (Louisiana Department of Public Safety, Louisiana)
Mr. John Conway (Massachusetts Department of State Police, Massachusetts)
Lt. Phillip Arriola (Detroit Police Department, Michigan)
Mr. Mark Greenwald (Michigan State University, Michigan)
Mr. Malcom Hall (Michigan Department of State Police, Michigan)
Mr. William Johnson (Michigan State University, Michigan)
Mr. John McClug (Wayne State University, Michigan)
Mr. Hiro Nakasone (Michigan State University, Michigan)
Ms. Marie Parrie (Michigan State University, Michigan)
Lt. Lonnie Smrkovski (Michigan Department of State Police, Michigan)
Dr. Oscar Tosi (Michigan State University, Michigan)
Ms. Linda Chiari (Voice Identification, Inc., Somerville, New Jersey)
Mr. William Kennedy (Essex County Prosecution Office, New Jersey)
Mr. Lawrence Kersta (Somerville, New Jersey)
Mr. Charles Lange (Bergen Co. Prosecution Office, New Jersey)
Mr. Steven Baymack (New York City Police Department, New York)
Mr. Edward Goutnick (Nassau Co. Police, New York)
Dr. John Black (Ohio State University, Ohio)
Mr. Peter Novosel (Youngstown Police Department, Ohio)
Dr. John Perkins (Ohio State University, Ohio)
Dr. John Swan (Harrisburg Community College, Pennsylvania)
Mr. William Anderson (South Carolina Law Enforcement Division, South Carolina)
Mr. Frederich Lundgren (ATF, Washington, D.C.)

In Argentina:

Dr. Mirta Morrone (Buenos Aires University)
Dr. Renato Segre (Buenos Aires University)

In Canada:

Mr. John Funk (Ministry of Solicitor General, Toronto)
Dr. Elaine Presman (Ottawa University)
Mr. Ken Taylor (RMP Headquarters, Ottawa)

In Italy:

Dr. Georgina Bordone (Galileo Ferraris Institute, Torino)
Dr. Raffaele Pisani (Galileo Ferraris Institute, Torino)
Dr. Gino Sacerdote (Galileo Ferraris Institute, Torino)

In Iran:

Lt. Javad Madadi (Interpol, Teheran)
Gen. Abbas Sarghi (Interpol, Teheran)

In Israel:

Inspector Shy Elal (Crime Laboratory, Jerusalem Police)
Dr. I. Tobin (Crime Laboratory, Jerusalem Police)

In Japan:

Mr. Seijo Fujima (Crime Laboratory, Tokyo Police)

In South Africa:

Dr. Len Jansen (Laboratory of Acoustics, Pretoria)

In addition to members and trainees of IAVI (including 18 persons holding
doctorates) the following scientists have expressed by letter or otherwise
their support for voice identification by aural and spectrographic examination of speech samples if properly used by trained examiners:

Dr. John Atkinson (USA)
Dr. John Cantlon (USA)
Dr. Leo Deal (USA)
Dr. Catherine Houlihan (USA)
Dr. Pal Kapur (USA)
Dr. Karl Kryter (USA)
Dr. Milton Muelder (USA)
Dr. Thomas Murray (USA)
Dr. Herbert Oyer (USA)

Dr. Boyd D. Roberts (USA)
Dr. Sadanah Singh (USA)
Dr. Dennis Tanner (USA)
Dr. C. E. Tomas (USA)
Dr. Peter Bloch (Brazil)
Dr. Bernard Vallancien (France)
Dr. Lucio Croato (Italy)
Dr. A. Caceres V. (Peru)
Dr. José Gisbert Alos (Spain)
Dr. George Perelló (Spain)

References

Aerospace Corporation. 1977. Speaker Identification. Program 7907 Final Report, No. ATR-77 (7617-07)-1. Aerospace Corporation, El Segundo, CA.

Atal, B. 1972. Automatic speaker recognition based on pitch contour. Journal of the Acoustical Society of America 52:1687-1697.

Atal, B. 1974. Effectiveness of linear prediction characteristics of speech wave for automatic speaker identification and verification. Journal of the Acoustical Society of America 55(6):1304-1312.

Atal B., and Schroeder, M. 1970. Adaptive predictive coding of speech signals. Bell System Technical Journal 49:1973-1986.

Barker, P. 1977. Presentation at the debate on "Voiceprints" organized by the Academy of Forensic Applications of Communication Sciences, December, Florida.

Becker, R. W., Clark, F. R., Poza, F., and Young, R. J. 1972. A Semiautomatic Speaker Recognition System. Stanford Research Institute Report No. 1363, Stanford, CA.

Black, J. W. 1937. The quality of a spoken vowel. Archives of Speech 2:7-27.

Black, J. W., Lashbrook, W., Nash E., Oyer, H., Pedrey, C., Tosi, O., and Truby, H. 1973. Reply to speaker identification by speech spectrograms: Some further observations. Journal of the Acoustical Society of America 54:535-537.

Bolt, R., Cooper, F., David E., Denes, P., Pickett, J., and Stevens, K. 1973. Speaker identification by speech spectrograms: Some further observations. Journal of the Acoustical Society of America 54:531-534.

Bordone, C., Dubes, R., Pisani, R., Sacerdote, G., and Tosi, O. 1974. Invariances of talkers' choral spectra. Paper presented at 87th meeting of the Acoustical Society of America, April 23-26, New York.

Bricker, P., and Pruzansky, S. 1966. Effect of stimulus content and duration on talker identification. Journal of the Acoustical Society of America 40:1441-1449.

Bricker, P., and Pruzansky, S. 1976. "Speaker Recognition." In N. Lass (ed.), Contemporary Issues in Experimental Phonetics, pp. 295-326. Academic Press, New York.

Coleman, R. 1973. Speaker identification in the absence of intersubject differences in glottal source characteristics. Journal of the Acoustical Society of America 53:1741-1743.

Daniloff, R. G., and Hammarberg, R. E. 1973. On definition of coarticulation. Journal of Phonetics 1:185-194.

Denes, P., and Pinson, E. 1963. The Speech Chain. Bell Telephone Laboratories, NJ.

Endress, W., Bambach, W., and Flosser, G. 1971. Voice spectrograms as function of age, voice disguise, and voice imitation. Journal of the Acoustical Society of America 49:1842-1848.

Gray, C. H., and Kopp, G. A. 1944. Voiceprint Identification. Bell Telephone Laboratories Report, pp. 1, 3, 13, 14. Bell Laboratories.

Greene, H. 1975. Voiceprint identification. The case in favor of admissibility. American Criminal Law Review 13:171.

Hair, G., and Rekieta, T. 1972. Speaker identification final report. Stanford Research Institute Report No. 1363. Stanford, CA.

Hazen, B. 1973. Effects of different phonetic contexts on spectrographic speaker identification. Journal of the Acoustical Society of America 54:650–660.

Hollien, H. 1977. Status report of "voiceprint" identification in the United States. Paper presented at the Second International Conference of Crime Countermeasures, Science and Engineering, July 25–29, Oxford, England.

Hollien, H., and Majewski, W. 1977. Speaker identification by long term spectra, under normal and distorted speech conditions. Journal of the Acoustical Society of America 62(4):975–980.

Hollien, H., and McGlone, R. 1976. The effect of disguise on "Voiceprint Identification." In Proceedings of the Carnahan Crime Countermeasures Conference, University of Kentucky. University of Kentucky Press, Lexington.

Holmgren, G. 1967. Physical and psychological correlates of speaker recognition. Journal of Speech and Hearing Research 10:57–66.

Houlihan, C. 1977. The effect of disguise on speaker identification from sound spectrograms. In Proceedings of the International Phonetic Sciences Congress, December, Miami, FL.

Jones, W. 1973. Danger—Voiceprints ahead. American Criminal Law Review 11:549–573.

Jones, W. 1974. Evidence vel non. The nonsense of voiceprint identification. Kentucky Law Journal 62:301–326.

Kersta, L. G. 1962a. Voiceprint identification. Nature 196:1253–1257.

Kersta, L. G. 1962b. Voiceprint infallibility. Paper presented at the November 1962 meeting of the Acoustical Society of America, Seattle, WA.

Ladefoged, P., and Vanderslice, R. 1967. The voiceprint mystique. Working Papers in Phonetics, Vol. 7. University of California, Los Angeles.

Li, K., and Hughes, G. 1974. Talker differences as they appear in correlation matrices of continuous speech spectra. Journal of the Acoustical Society of America 55:883–887.

McGehee, F. 1937. The reliability of the identification of the human voice. Journal of General Psychology 17:249–271.

McGehee, F. 1944. An experimental study of voice recognition, Journal of General Psychology 31:53–65.

Murphy, T. 1977. Presentation to the Committee on Speech Spectrograms of the National Academy of Sciences, Washington, D.C.

Papçun, G., and Ladefoged, P. 1973. Two voiceprint cases. Paper presented at the 85th meeting of the Acoustical Society of America, November 10–15, Los Angeles.

Pollack, I., Pickett, J., and Sumby, W. 1954. On the identification of speakers by voice. Journal of the Acoustical Society of America 26:403–406.

Potter, R., Kopp, G., and Green, H. 1947. Visible Speech. Van Nostrand, New York. Reprinted (1966) by Dover, New York.

Poza, F. 1974. Voiceprint identification: Its forensic application. In Proceedings of the Carnahan Crime Countermeasures Conference, University of Kentucky. University of Kentucky Press, Lexington.

Presti, A. J. 1966. High-speed sound spectrograph. Journal of the Acoustical Society of America 40:628-634.

Pruzanski, S. 1966. Pattern matching procedure for automatic talker recognition. Journal of the Acoustical Society of America 35:354-358.

Reich, A., Moll, K., and Curtis, J. 1976. Effects of selected vocal disguises upon spectrographic speake identification. Journal of the Acoustical Society of America 60:919-925.

Rothman, H. 1977. Presentation at the debate on "Voiceprints" organized by the Academy of Forensic Applications of Communication Sciences, December, Florida.

Shafer, R.L., and Rabiner, L. 1975. Digital representation of speech signals. Proceedings of the IEEE 63:662-667.

Siegel, D. 1976. Cross-examination of a "Voiceprint" expert. Journal of Criminal Defense 2:79-116.

Smrkovski, L. 1976. Study of speaker identification by aural and visual examination of non-contemporary speech samples. Journal of Official Analytical Chemists 59:927-931.

Solzhenitsyn, A. 1968. The First Circle. Translation from Russian by T. Whitney. Harper & Row, New York.

Starr, S., Metz, C., Lusted, L., and Goodenough, D. 1975. Visual detection and localization of radiographic images. Radiology 116:553-558.

Stevens, K. N., House, A. S., and Paul, A. P. 1966. Acoustical description of syllabic nuclei: An interpretation in terms of a dynamic model of articulation. Journal of the Acoustical Society of America 40:123-132.

Stevens, K. N., Williams, C. E., Carbonell, J. R., and Woods, B. 1968. Speaker authentication and identification: A comparison of spectrographic and auditory presentation of speech material. Journal of the Acoustical Society of America 44:1596-1607.

Swetts, J. 1973. The relative operating characteristics in psychology. Science 182:990-1000.

Su, L., and Fu, K. 1973. Automatic speaker identification using nasal spectra and nasal coarticulation as acoustic clues. Report from the Purdue University School of Electrical Engineering, TR-EE 73-33. Air Force Office of Scientific Research Grant 69-1776. Purdue University, Lafayette, IN.

Su, L., Li, S., and Fu, K. 1974. Identification of speakers by use of nasal coarticulation. Journal of the Acoustical Society of America 56:1876-1882.

Tarnoczy, T. 1958. Determination du spectre de la parole avec une méthode nouvelle. Acustica 8:392-395.

Tosi, O. 1967. Report to the Michigan Department of State Police. (Also presented at 1968 International Congress of Logopedics and Phoniatrics, Paris, France.)

Tosi, O. 1973. Report to LEAA. September, Michigan.

Tosi, O. 1977. Presentation at the debate on "Voiceprints" organized by the Academy of Forensic Applications of Communication Sciences, December, Florida.

Tosi, O., and Greenwald, M. 1978. Voice identification by subjective methods of minority group voices. Paper presented at the 7th Meeting of the International Association of Voice Identification, New Orleans, LA.

Tosi, O., Oyer, H., Lashbrook, W., Pedrey, C., Nicol, J., and Nash, E. 1972. Experiment on voice identification. Journal of the Acoustical Society of America 51:2030–2043.

Tosi, O., Pisani, R., Dubes, R., and Jaim, A. 1977. An objective method of voice identification. Proceedings of the International Phonetic Sciences Congress, December, Miami, Florida.

Truby, H. 1977. The application of voiceprint analysis to speaker individuation. Paper presented at the Second International Conference of Crime Countermeasures, Sciences and Engineering, July 25–29, Oxford, England.

Voiers, W. 1964. Perceptual bases of speaker identity. Journal of the Acoustical Society of America 36:1065–1073.

Wolf, J. 1972. Efficient acoustic parameters for speaker recognition. Journal of the Acoustical Society of America 51:2044–2056.

Young, M., and Campbell, R. 1967. Effects of contexts on talker identification. Journal of the Acoustical Society of America 42:1250–1254.

Index